The Bible On
Light

The Bible

on

Light

by L. SIBUM

Translated by F. Vander Heijden, O. Praem.

ST. NORBERT ABBEY PRESS
De Pere, Wisconsin
U. S. A.
1966

163444

Nihil obstat:

Samuel D. Jadin, O. Praem.
Censor deputatus

Imprimatur:

†Stanislaus V. Bona, D.D.
Bishop of Green Bay
January 24, 1966

The *Nihil obstat* and *Imprimatur* are a declaration that a book or pamphlet is considered free from doctrinal or moral error. It is not implied that those who have granted the *Nihil obstat* and *Imprimatur* agree with the contents, opinions or statements expressed.

Originally published as
De Bijbel over Licht 1962
Roermond and Maaseik, J. J. Romen & Zonen, 1962

Library of Congress catalogue card number: 66 - 16992

Printed in the United States of America
ST. NORBERT ABBEY PRESS
De Pere, Wisconsin

CONTENTS

FOREWORD

Light, splendor and like words appear frequently in the religious literature of all peoples. They are also found in the Bible. On the first page of the Bible we read that the Almighty commenced his great works with the creation of light, "the eldest daughter at God's feet" as the Dutch poet Vondel says; by creating light he instituted alternation of day and night. On the last page we read that earthly light gives way to the superior light of a new creation, the light which unceasingly shines in the holy city of the new Jerusalem.

Between this first and last page, between this beginning and fulfillment, we meet the word light many times: earthly light, but in this we discern the wonderful light of the new creation. This new creation does not begin with the end of this world, nor is its light only lit on the youngest day. This light dawns and the new creation begins when the Lord of glory reveals himself to us, testifying of himself: "I am the light of the world."

Christ stands as the central figure in Holy Scripture. All rays of light point to him and coverage in him; they originate from him and meet in him. Whoever opens his eyes and his heart to it is transformed into the light which he himself is: "For once you were darkness, but now you are light in the Lord."

In this book the author has tried to collect what
is said about light in the Old and in the New Testament. He would be happy if other people were
persuaded to join him in this quest, which although
not easy, does bring many enriching surprises. These
notes attempt to be an easy guide to the chief sites,
pointing out the most interesting particulars, and
sometimes drawing attention to territories which
must still be reconnoitred and where one could
perhaps find an object for preoccupation.

No guide can save us the labor involved in such
a quest. But he can lighten it. At every turn he
reminds the pilgrims of Israel's journey toward the
promised land; at every turn he points out to them
the resplendent goal which is worth all the exertion;
at every turn he shows them the light that the Father
in his infinite love has shown to us, the light which
we welcome thankfully and jubilantly in the Easter
wake of our earthly life: **Lumen Christi, Deo gratias!**

The third general meeting of the World Council
of Churches, in the last months of 1961, chose the
words of Scripture where Jesus calls himself the
light of the world as the chief topic of its discussions.
Our book is, in a somewhat modified form, an essay
which was written on that occasion and which
appeared in **Het Christelijk Oosten en Hereniging**
(Vol. 14, numbers 1 and 2).

It is a matter of joy and gratitude for us that our
essay in this modified form may enable others to
walk along these biblical paths of light.

PART I

THE OLD TESTAMENT ON LIGHT

Texts about light are spread throughout the books of the Bible. In the New Testament the true light reveals its full splendor. But it has already forecast this splendor in the Old Testament. Thus the brightness of day is preceded by an enchanting dawn in which the light slowly blossoms and by doing so gradually spreads before our gaze its wonderful composition and richness. Therefore, we will first see what the Old Testament says about light. This will enable us to prepare for the overwhelming splendor which meets us in the New Testament.

YAHWEH ENVELOPS HIMSELF
IN LIGHT AS IN A MANTLE

Light and fire strike us as mysterious, indescribable, almost immaterial entities. But at the same time they force themselves upon us as tangible and inescapable realities which may be valuable or, as is often the case with fire, formidable realities. Without fire and light there is no warmth, no life, no growth, no activity. Quite naturally, light especially becomes the symbol of whatever is dear and necessary to man: guidance, virtue, happiness; darkness becomes the symbol of things which man abhors and avoids: error, sin, calamity.

We must point out that the details of these symbolisms, comparisons and metaphors of light and darkness follow different lines with different people. In the language of the Old Testament light does not indicate eyesight nor intelligence. In our language however this happens so commonly, that the originally metaphoric character of this usage is seldom understood.

Because man represented the deity to himself as unintelligible and as the indispensable cause of all good things and as a terrifying power, it was logical

that he would represent the deity as enveloped in
fire and light, or that he would even identify the
deity with them; we find these fire-gods, light-gods,
sun-gods, moon-gods and star-gods or — goddesses
throughout mythology.

1. Light as God's creature

In the Old Testament[1] fire and light are often
mentioned in connection with God's nature and action. This is also done in the religious language of
the Egyptians, the Babylonians, the Persians. But
this similarity is superficial. The Israelite does not
think, at least not in the usual way of speaking, of
light as an oscillation of ether molecules, and darkness for him is not merely absence of light. Even
though the sun radiates light and warmth (Ps. 19:7;
Sir. 42:16; 43:2-5; cf. Is. 18:4), it is not thought of as
the source of daylight. In the creation narrative of
Genesis we meet sunless days: daylight is already
there before the sun is created. Light and darkness
are independent entities. God separated them in the
beginning. He allows them alternately to go out
over the earth in a constant succession of day and
night. After having fulfilled their task they withdraw
into the space which God provided for each of them
and which he alone knows. After them he formed

[1] The reader can easily check the references in Holy
Scripture in an English translation. For those who use the
original text and the old translations it did not seem necessary to point out the numerous different readings which
may be found there, especially in the Psalms, Sirach
(=Ecclesiasticus) and other books of the Old Testament.
In translations of the Bible these differences are usually
mentioned.

the heavenly bodies and clothed them with sparkling light: sun, moon and stars. In their constant revolutions, according to the rhythm and the course God prescribed for them, they are the pride and glory of the firmament (Ps. 8:2-5; Sir. 43:1, 8, 9). But they also received a definite task from God, namely, to determine the duration, the succession and the regularity of days, months and seasons: to form an agricultural and festival calendar for man (Gen. 1:3-5, 14-18; Job 26:10; 38:19-20; Ps. 104:19-23; 136:7-9; Sir. 43:1-11; Bar. 3:33; Dan. 2:22).

Perhaps another way of thinking is to be found in some texts (Sir. 33:7; Is. 60:19) in which the sun is really the source of light. But it is mostly the translations which speak clearly in this sense. In the original text we find the meaning that the sun is filled with light and that its course determines the duration or the festival character of the day. For God made "the sun to rule over the day" (Ps. 136:8).

Nevertheless, all biblical authors agree on one point: the light which meets our eyes is a creature; an enchanting, mysterious creature to be sure, but a creature just the same. This is true too, for lightning, which is sometimes simply called "light" (Job 36:32; 37:3, 11, 15) or is described as a flashing arrow in God's hand (Ps. 29:7; 77:18; Hab. 3:11; Zech. 9:14). God calls it and sends it out as the messenger of his terrifying power.

For Israel, therefore, there can be no question at all of identifying Yahweh with the light we perceive with our eyes. The doctrine that God calls the

heavenly bodies and the light into existence with
one single word, and that he has given them a role
which is subservient to man, is stressed so forcefully
in the Bible, that this is undoubtedly intended as a
resolute rejection of the cult of sun, moon and stars
by the people around Israel (Deut. 4:19; 17:3; Job
31:26; Wisd. 13:2; Jer. 8:2; Ezek. 8:16). But being
God's creatures they do point toward the Father of
the lights (Jas. 1:17). Indeed, God often takes light
and splendor into his service to teach man in a
visible way something about his transcendent and
invisible greatness. This has been expressed in a
surprising way by the psalmist who, following the
narrative of Genesis, sings about the wonders of
creation. When God's powerful command "Let there
be light" evokes light from the dark abyss, it looks
to the poet as if the Creator envelops himself in a
mantle of light: "O Lord my God, thou art very great!
Thou art clothed with honor and majesty, who
coverest thyself with light as with a garment" (Ps.
102:1-2). We often see him described as surrounded
by clouds in which lightning flashes, as enveloped
in light (Ps. 76:5; Hab. 3:4), as accompanied by —
personified — light (Ps. 43:3; Dan. 2:12), or as surrounded by flames and fire (Gen. 15:17; Ex. 3:2; cf.
Acts 2:3).

2. The column of fire which guided God's people

When the Israelites marched from Egypt toward
the promised land the Lord "went before by day
in a pillar of cloud to lead them along the way, and
by night in a pillar of fire to give them light, that
they might travel by day and by night. The pillar

of cloud by day and the pillar of fire by night did not depart from before the people" (Ex. 13:21-22; 14:19-20, 24; Num. 14:14). In this way the earliest, that is the Yahwistic, tradition teaches us about the exodus. Later texts repeatedly mention this wonderful event (Ex. 40:34-38; Num. 9:15-23; 10:11-12; Deut. 1:33; Neh. 9:12, 19; Ps. 78:14; 105:39; Wisd. 10:17; 18:3). There may be many small differences, but all testimonies agree that Yahweh himself, enveloped in light, guided his people through the desert. He hid himself in the light and at the same time he revealed himself in it, and so guided Israel toward the holy land.

At times the restoration after the exile and the messianic salvation are pictured as a new exodus from Egypt, a thought which still resounds in our Easter and baptism liturgy. Again Yahweh marches at the head of his people and guides them by the light of his glory; again there appear "a cloud by day, and smoke and the shining of a flaming fire by night" (Is. 4:5; cf. 42:15-16; 52:12; Bar. 5:9). Moreover there are some texts in which what is said about God is ascribed to the personified divine Wisdom: "She led them out on their miraculous journey, affording them shelter by day and starry radiance by night" (Wisd. 10:17; cf. Sir. 24:4).

3. Thunder and lightning

It is known that God's visible interventions are often accompanied by thunder and lightning. The most impressive display of power undoubtedly is the one described as a prelude to the legislation on Mount Sinai (Ex. 19:16-19; cf. 20:18-21), mentioned

many times afterward. Resourceful scholars interpret
this as if Yahweh originally had been the god of
fire and thunderstorms of one or other nomadic
clan, or of the Canaanites. The truth is that Yahweh,
the creator of the universe, also disposes of thunder
and lightning at will (Ps. 29), sometimes to inspire
people with awe for his law and majesty, as in the
texts which we have quoted, and elsewhere (Ps.
18:8-16; 77:17-20; 97:2-5) to sweep away his enemies
from the earth and to help his servants.[2]

---

[2] Whether parts of pagan religious literature have been
taken into the Bible is another question. In ancient times
holy places of Canaan were assimilated into the service of
Israel's God. The sanctuary where "Yahweh is seated upon
the Cherubim" shows many similarities to the sacrificial
service of a Canaanite temple. In the same way, many
centuries later, Christians sometimes met in what formerly
were temples of idols. They did not immediately design a
new style for their churches and religious representations
(the Good Shepherd, for example, is painted as Orpheus,
Apollo or Hermes Kriophoros). In both cases people were
led, more or less consciously, by the thought that all the
noble things with which the pagans wished to honor their
gods belong only to the one true God. Christians have
Christianized titles and invocations used in the cults of light
and sun, and have applied them in their liturgy to Christ,
the true light (see many examples in F. J. Dolger, *Sol
Salutis 2*, Münster in W. 1936, p. 1-43). In the same way
a sacred author may have borrowed something from the
Canaanites or others, in order to express his own thoughts.
Something like this is often said to have taken place in
our psalm 29: a hymn, they say, originally sung in honor
of a god of the tempest which, in modified form, was
listed among the psalms. This however is very difficult to
prove. The topic of this psalm — Yahweh's glory appearing
in a thunderstorm — is often found in Holy Scripture.
According to critics it is a feature of the "sacerdotal"
tradition.

2

THE LIGHT OF YAHWEH'S GLORY

Thunderstorms, as an accompaniment of God, are undoubtedly also associated with the "glory of Yahweh." In Hebrew this is indicated by the word **kâbôd**. It appears 149 times in the Old Testament; 29 times it is used in the fixed expression "the glory of Yahweh." The original meaning of the word is probably heaviness, or weight, which gradually comes to mean preponderance, wealth, honor, glory. The Septuagint usually translates it by **doxa;** in the texts just mentioned it is always translated in this way. This Greek word has several meanings, such as opinion, fame, honor; but, especially in the texts from the hellenistic period it indicates a flashing or radiance. In our case it must have this last meaning. Some scholars are of the opinion that "radiance" is the fundamental meaning of the Hebrew term.[3] In any case, wherever the glory of Yahweh is men-

---

[3] See Koehler-Baumgartner, *Lexicon in V. T. Libros*, Leiden 1958, s. v.; P. van Imschoot, "Heerlijkheid," in *Bijbels Woordenboek* 2, Roermond-Maaseik 1954 - 1957, c. 670-674. In texts where the meaning of *kabod* or *doxa* evidently is as we have explained it, we find some translations, even by the same translator, which differ: *magnificence, glory, majesty*, etc. In all cases we have used the term "glory."

tioned in Scripture, originally at least it meant this
radiance of fire or light, in which God hides and
makes his power felt. Although in this respect it
is similar to the column of fire which guided Israel
through the desert, still in many texts it is dis-
tinguished from it. The clearest description of it is
the following: "The glory of the Lord settled on
Mount Sinai, and the cloud covered it six days; and
on the seventh day he called to Moses out of the
midst of the cloud. Now the appearance of the
glory of the Lord was like a devouring fire on the
top of the mountain in the sight of the people of
Israel" (Ex. 24:16-17; Deut. 5:22-26). The fire, which
here blazes up in a cloud, elsewhere consumes the
sacrifice of Aaron (Lev. 9:6, 23-24) and destroys the
evildoers (Num. 16:19, 35). In connection with such
fire we necessarily think of the thunderstorm which
usually accompanies the solemn appearance of
Yahweh, especially because other texts also suggest
the same idea: "The voice of Yahweh is upon the
waters! The God of glory the Lord, thunders, upon
many waters!" (Ps. 29:3; 97:1-6; Ezek. 1:4, 13).

1. Glory far and glory near

In many texts the glory of God seems less clearly
connected with thunder and lightning, although
there are still some traces of them, as e.g. the cloud
which accompanies it or the awe it inspires.

In some of those texts — which may represent the
earliest tradition — the glory which surrounds
Yahweh is so absolutely unearthly that no man can
behold its full splendor without dying. Moses, as

a special favor, is allowed to see this glory from behind after it had passed him while God had covered his eyes. In other words, even being allowed to see the mitigated splendor of the outer edge of God's glory is an exceptional favor (Ex. 33:18-23; cf. Is. 6:3, 5).

In other texts however, more closely related to the above quoted description (Ex. 24:16-17), God's glory is a visible form in which the unapproachable God reveals himself to Israel, while he nevertheless remains hidden from all perception. Enveloped in a cloud the glory of God descends upon the people (Ex. 16:10). From within this glory God makes his will known and grants his favors, in or near the tent of meeting (Ex. 29:43-44; Num. 14:10; 17:7; 20:6). It is the reflection of this glory — though it is not mentioned by name — which made the face of Moses radiant after God had spoken to him (Ex. 34:29-35; cf. 2 Cor. 3:7-11, 18; 4:6). As it filled the newly built tent according to Ex. 40:34-35, so it also filled the newly built temple and takes possession of it (1 Kings 8:10-11). Ezekiel sees the glory of Yahweh rising up from its place in the Holy of Holies and departing from the temple, which had been sullied by the idolatry of Judah. But he knows that one day it will return in order to dwell in a new temple amid a sanctified people (Ezek. 8:4; 9:3; 10:4, 18, 19; 43:1-4). The visions of this prophet describe this glory as surrounded by every tangible phenomena. But they give us a very spiritualized version of it. It is invisible, always present in the sanctuary, without being confined to it.

There is no contradiction between the two groups
of texts which we have mentioned; we should consider them connected. Although the glory as an ex-
ternal manifestation of Yahweh usually resides in
the sanctuary of Israel, it also shows itself outside:
"in the land of the Chaldeans by the river Chebar"
(Ezek. 1:3-4; 8:1-4; 10:10-22) and "the earth shone
with his glory" as in the last times it reverts to the
people of God (43:2). Vice versa, although the unearthly glory, before which even the seraphs cover
their face, fills the whole earth, and though it is
outlined against the vaults of heaven (Num. 14:21;
Ps. 19:2; 72:19; Hab. 2:14), still it shows itself to
Isaiah in a temple, which is an idealized temple
of Jerusalem, the heavenly model of this temple
(Is. 6:1-4). Unless Yahweh prevents it, man would
die beholding this glory. Even the earthly form in
which Yahweh's glory appears is awe inspiring:
wherever it is seen man falls on his face to the earth
and keeps a respectful distance from it (Ex. 34:29-30;
40:34-35; Num. 20:6; 1 Kings 8:11; Ezek. 1:28; 45:3).

Is this glory perhaps the heavenly glory itself,
only tempered by and enveloped in a cloud in order
to make it bearable for the human eye? It is better
to say that just as the earthly house of Yahweh is a
copy of the heavenly model (Ex. 25:9, 40; 1 Chron.
28:19; Ps. 29:2, 7; Is. 6:1-4; cf. Heb. 8:2-5; Rev. 15:5)
so also the earthly appearance of his glory is the
reflection and imitation of Yahweh's heavenly glory.

This we conclude especially from the visions of

Ezekiel. In his description the prophet relies on tradition. The glory in which God came down upon Sinai, in which he wished to speak to Israel and in which he wished to be reconciled to his people by the sacrificial blood on the day of atonement (Lev. 16), that glory as it rested in the darkness of the Holy of Holies, between the Cherubim above the Ark, this very glory shows itself to the seer (Ezek. 1:3-28). Surely, it is here a resplendent, "nearly human" figure and it moves in a human way: it rises up, it settles down, it comes and goes. The Ark on which it sits has been transformed into a wonderfully movable wagon and the Cherubim which carry it are filled with spirit and life. Thus this glory comes hurtling down from the north into the country of the Chaldeans, in the midst of a blaze of fire, lightning and thunder. But although it appears as living with its surroundings, yet it is Yahweh's glory as we know it from other texts (Ezek. 24:16-17 etc.).

Concerning this glory and many particulars which he notices in it (Ezek. 1:4, 5, 13, 22, 26, 27), Ezekiel is taught that it is only a likeness or a reflection of the indescribable glory which resides above the firmament (cf. 1:22 "the likeness of a firmament"), the outward appearance in which God reveals himself to man. It was something that looked like the glory of Yahweh, the prophet says at the end of his description; literally, "Such was the appearance of the likeness of Yahweh's glory" (1:28). Elsewhere he says (8:4): "And behold, the glory of the God of

Israel was there, like the vision that I saw in the plain."[4]

2. The glory in the future restoration

In Ezekiel's description of the future restoration the glory of Yahweh again dwells in a new temple among his chosen people (Ezek. 43:1-7). We see the same with the prophets and other pious people. The column of fire belongs to the messianic intervention, where God establishes the truly chosen people. In the same way the glory of Yahweh belongs to it; it is the center and source of unity and indestructible life for this people. Probably this salutary event is already prophesied in the cry of the Seraphim before God's throne: "the whole earth is full of his glory" (Is. 6:3; cf. Jn. 12:41). The inhabitants of heaven behold a reality which those who dwell on earth can only desire and pray for.[5] The message of Isaiah, that "the Holy One of Israel," alone, will be the exalted One, is in an incomparable manner summarized by the Seraphim in this vision of the vocation of the prophet.

The many texts in which future redemptive intervention of God is unmistakably described as a new exodus from Egypt (as in the second part of Isaiah) or in another way, speak a language which is even

[4] The same word *mar'eh* (appearance, countenance, exterior) occurs 15 times in the first chapter of Ezekiel, always with this meaning.

[5] W. Eichrodt, *Theologie des Alten Testaments II*, Leipzig 1935, p. 10, in his thorough study about the glory of Yahweh pp. 9-12.

clearer. The new world which Yahweh will create;
the decisive intervention of his omnipotence (cf.
Num. 14:21; Hab. 2:14); the victory of the kingdom;
the salvation which the Servant of Yahweh brings
about for Israel and for the nations; the mercy of
God who saves all sinful mankind and takes it up
again into his friendship, — all this is summarized
here as the resplendent dawn of Yahweh's glory over
the holy city and over God's elect. This glory
envelops them and permeates them, so much so
that they themselves radiate God's glory (Ps. 57:6;
72:19; Sir. 36:12, 13; Is. 40:5; 49:5; 59:19; 60:1-3; cf.
60:19-20 and Rev. 21:11, 23-26; Is. 66:18; Bar. 4:24,
37; 5:7; cf. 2 Macc. 2:8-10).

The dawn of Yahweh's glory takes a special form
in Daniel. In his vision of the Ancient of Days and
the Son of Man (Dan. 7:9-27) we can in many in-
stances trace the influence of Ezekiel. In the
writings of the latter, the glory of Yahweh takes an
almost human form. In Daniel we read: "And behold,
with the clouds of heaven there came one like a
son of man, and he came to the Ancient of Days and
was presented before him. And to him was given
dominion and glory and kingdom, that all peoples,
nations and languages should serve him" (Dan.
7:13-14). The enigmatic being who appears in the
shape of a man and who nevertheless is shown as
transcending whatever is human, undoubtedly is the
Messiah, who in his person represents the saintly
people of the Most High (Dan. 7:18, 22, 27). To
him therefore is also given the glory, together with

the dominion and the everlasting kingship over the
whole world.[6] God's glory is present on earth in the
figure of this Son of Man and in his messianic reign
(cf. Mt. 24:30; Mk. 13:16; Lk. 21:27). The glory
accompanies the eternal kingship with which God has
vested him. It stands radiating in the Holy of Holies
of the messianic time (Dan. 9:24); elsewhere in the
Bible it is described as enveloping in its radiance
the earthly seat of God, the Ark, or the heavenly
throne of the King, Yahweh of the hosts, in his holy
temple (Is. 6:1-5; Bar. 5:1-4; Ezek. 43:5-7; cf. Wisd.
9:10).

3. The glory as the sign of Israel's God
and of his exalted power

We have outlined the meaning of Yahweh's glory:
it is the "apparel of radiating splendor in which
Yahweh envelops himself and reveals himself." The
term also has another meaning when applied to God.
It often indicates his exalted power or, as a sign
of this, a miracle (Ps. 66:2; 96:3; 145:5-10; Wisd. 9:11;
Is. 42:8; 48:11). If we keep in mind that the glory
of Yahweh originally was connected with a violent
display of power in thunder and lightning, we understand at once that this meaning is close to the

---

[6] Our text, which belongs to the Aramaic part of Daniel,
does not use the word *kabod* (this occurs only once in the
Hebraic parts of Daniel, in 11:30), but *Yekar*, which originally also means heaviness, weight; secondarily it means
honor, splendor, glory. In Daniel it occurs very often in
connection with domination and kingship. — About the
Son of Man in Daniel see P. van Imschoot and J. Nelis in
Bijbels Woordenboek 2, c. 1118-1119 (see remark 3).

original one; it accompanies it and is embodied in it. This is especially the case in the fourth gospel, as we shall see repeatedly later.

Because God and his glory are so closely connected, it also happens that the word indicates God himself, e.g. where he is called "the glory of Israel" (Ps. 106:20; Jer. 2:11; cf. Rom. 1:23; 2 Pet. 1:17).

There is no need to speak about this and other meanings of the word. We must however consider the many texts in the Old Testament where light is a symbol of a divine reality, or where the term is applied to this reality in a comparative or metaphoric way.

3

THE LIGHT IN GOD'S HOUSE

In Yahweh's temple beside the lights which were needed for practical purposes there was also a special light which was kept burning for him. In this chapter we will examine the nature and significance of this special light, which at first sight would seem superfluous.

1. A holy light

In the texts which speak about this special light it is evident that the number and form of lamps and candelabra have changed in the course of time. Their number and shape are evidently incidental. In the sanctuary of Shilo one lamp burned (1 Sam. 3:3; cf. Ex. 27:21-22); in the temple of Solomon stood ten candelabra (1 Kings 17:49; 2 Kings 4:7; cf. Jer. 52:19); in the temple of Zerubbabel there was one candelabrum with seven arms, as one was also ascribed to the tabernacle of Moses (Ex. 25:31-40; 37:17-24; 40:24-25; Lev. 24:1-4; Num. 8:1-4; I Macc. 1:21; 4:49). This candelabrum with seven arms probably looked different from the sevenfold candelabrum

which was shown to Zechariah (4:2, 3, 10) in a
vision.[7]

In all this, one fact is evident: as long as Yahweh
has a definite abode in the holy land, from the
period of the Judges until the fall of Jerusalem in
70 A.D., a special light burned in· his abode. This
light was considered to be very holy, as we can see
from the texts quoted. The flame of this lamp of
God was to be fed with the very finest olive oil.
The Aaronitic priests had to keep it burning before
Yahweh's face. It stood upon a chandelier cast of
native gold. In a word, every feature of this light
was designated by God himself: "A statute for ever
to be observed throughout their generations" (Ex.
27:21).

Possibly in later times this light burned day and
night. This is testified to by Hecataeus of Abdera
in Flavious Josephus (c. Ap. I. 22) — really the
pseudo-Hecataeus toward the end of the third century
B.C.[8] — while according to Josephus himself (Ant.

[7] The candalabrum which Zechariah describes was very
probably a gigantic chalice, a wide semispheric cup, resting
on a high stem. The seven lamps were arranged on the
broad rim of the cup at equal distances from one another.
Cf. a picture in Galling, *Biblisches Reallexikon*, Tübingen
1937, p. 348. On candelabrum and lamps see also A. van
den Born, in *Bijbels Woordenboek 2*, c. 913 and 990-991
(remark 3); Wright Houwaard, *De Bijbel ontdekt in Aarde
en Steen 2*, Baarn 1960, pp. 226, 247 and picture 214 (the
sevenfold candelabrum on the triumphal arch of Tite).

[8] Schürer, *Geschichte des jüdischen Volkes III* 4, Leipzig
1909, pp. 603-608.

III. 8:3) three of the seven lamps remained burning by day. But in the earlier days this was surely not the case: the light burned only by night.

2. Significance of the holy light

Josephus really does not give an explanation of the significance of this light. He speaks only about the number of lamps, and this was considered incidental and had often been changed. In one text he says very wisely — speaking about the second temple — that there were seven lamps because seven was a holy number to the Jews (Bell. VII 5:5). But elsewhere he states that the seven lamps represented the seven planets (Ant. III. 7:7). Philo considers the lamps to be a symbol of the heavenly bodies (Vita Mos. III. 10; Qu. in Ex. II. 71). Many later Jewish writers attribute such a cosmic meaning to the lamps. Some scholars of our day think that in the temple of ·Solomon there was a double representation of the seven planets of the old astronomy. They add to the five chandeliers on the right and to the five chandeliers on the left the two big columns of Jakin and Boaz (1 Kings 7:21) as symbols of sun and moon; this seems to be a labored calculation!

These cosmic explanations have no foundation in Holy Scripture, not even in 1 Kings 8:12 brought into accord with the Septuagint: "Yahweh has set the sun in the heavens, but has said that he would dwell in thick darkness"; thus Solomon expresses his grateful admiration for the fact that Yahweh graciously deigned to dwell in the new temple. Yahweh, who suspended the sun in the heavens,

himself deigns to dwell in the darkness of the sanctuary. This darkness reminds Solomon of the cloud
in which God once marched before his people
through the desert or of the thunderclouds in which
the glory of Yahweh appeared. It is this glory which
is said to be present in the cloud and to fill the
temple (1 Kings 8:10-11). Nothing is said about the
holy light, supposedly a symbol of the sun. It cannot
be a symbol of the sun, because originally it was a
night light.

When it burned only at night, this was in accord
with the Israelitic or even generally-Semitic idea of
a temple. This is the house of God: it has a hearth,
namely, the altar on which the fire is always burning
(Lev. 6:5-6). It has a light which is lit in the evening
and extinguished in the morning. A place where
there is no light is considered as not inhabited; it is
a desert (Jer. 25:10-11; cf. Rev. 18:23). Therefore the
light tended by the priests is Israel's solemn acknowledgment that Yahweh dwells in their midst; on
Yahweh's side it is a solemn testimony that he resides
graciously with his people and that he surrounds it
with his constant providence. It is possible that this
divine care is also expressed in the form of the
candelabrum with seven arms: a stylized almond
tree. One of the names of this tree is the Hebrew
shâqed, which means "the alert" or "the vigilant"
(cf. Jer. 1:11-12), and the description of the candelabra (Ex. 25:31-36) exactly supposes this name.

When Zechariah in 519 B.C. describes the restoration after the exile in strongly messianic colors,

he summarizes the whole cult of the future in the image of the sevenfold candelabrum (Zech. 4:1-6a, 10b-14. Read 6b-10a: "This is the word, etc." after 4:14). On either side two olive trees provide oil for the lamps. This means that the cult is entrusted to two dignitaries who had been anointed with oil: a king and a high priest. In their fraternal cooperation they are a prefiguration of the messianic priesthood and kingship (cf. Jer. 33:14-26, a text which under influence of Zechariah and others completes a prophecy of Jeremiah, 23:5-6; cf. also Zech. 3:8; 6:12-13). The seven lamps of the chandelier are the image of the omniscient and ever vigilant providence of God for his people 2 Chron. 16:9; Job 29:2-3; Ps. 33:12-19; Zech. 3:9).

The holy light therefore symbolized the acknowledgment of God's people, by their constant cult, that Yahweh resides in a special way among them; at the same time it was assurance from Yahweh that he would ever keep watch in careful love over his people (Zech. 2:14-15; Rev. 1:12-20; 5:6; 11:4).

This symbolism of light is based upon some of the many comparisons we find in Holy Scripture; these will claim our attention in the following chapters.

4

MAGNIFICENT AND
BENEFICENT LIGHT

Since we will speak about the term light as used in comparison and metaphor, the reader must remember that it is impossible to draw a sharp line between some biblical concepts. Happiness, life, revelation and law are themselves lights inasmuch as they are a gift of the light which is God's graciousness. The light of virtue and righteousness again is the light of God's law and revelation in actual practice. Our classification intends to give a better survey of these different concepts.

1. The light of the eyes

In the Old Testament the light of the eyes does not mean eyesight, but the splendor shining from the eyes upon the surroundings, just as it radiates from the celestial bodies. This light shines from man's eyes as long as he is alive, and especially when he is happy (1 Sam. 14:27-29; Ezra 9:8; Tob. 10:4; Ps. 6:8; 13:4; 19:9; 38:11; Prov. 29:13; Sir. 34:17; Bar. 1:12; 3:14). The eyes are like lamps and it is no wonder that in Zechariah (4:10) lamps are said to be the image of God's eyes (Ps. 90:8; Prov. 15:30; Mt. 6:22; Lk. 11:34-36).

If a man is glad, his countenance is radiant (Ps.
34:6; Eccles.); a bright, merry glance is usually the
reflection and expression of a generous disposition.[9]
When a man is in need of mercy or help, he hopes
that someone (Job 29:24; Prov. 16:15), especially
God (Num. 6:25; Ps. 4:7; 31:17; 44:4; 67:2; 80:4;
89:16; 119:135; Dan. 9:17) will show "the light of his
face" or that he will make "his face shine over him."

Nothing is more natural than that a generous disposition or beneficence itself came to be called light.

According to our view the light of the eyes could
also be that which is destined for the eyes. Perhaps
this is not true for the authors of the Old Testament.
Of course, they knew the reality meant here; but
they would have described it differently.

2. Light as revelation and guidance

No darkness can remain before God for he who
creates the light does not derive it from someone
else (Job 12:22; 34:21-23; Ps. 139:11-12). Man however is dependent on the light which God grants
him. It is something we notice first and most clearly;
it enables us to see things around us in their true

[9] We could also refer to the Hebraic text of Sir. 7:24, where
the father is exhorted to watch over the purity (literally:
the flesh) of his daughters and not to let his face radiate
over them too much i.e. not to deal with them too playfully.
In 13:26 and 35:38 a "radiating face" is mentioned (I. Lévi,
The Hebrew Text of the Book of Ecclesiasticus, Leiden 1904,
reprinted 1951, pp. 10, 21, 36: chap. 7:24; 13:25; 35:9). The
Greek text and the modern translations at least give the
correct meaning when they say: a glad or merry face.

form. Therefore in Scripture whatever is obviously known or is made known is compared to a light (Ps. 37:6; Hos. 6:5); whatever makes us see the nature and significance of things is also referred to as a light.

Instruction about hidden things, which God gives to his prophets (Dan. 2:22), the judgment which he passes (Is. 51:4), or (Ps. 90:8) the bundle of rays which he sends out over the actions of man[10] — all these Scripture compares to light.

Only when there is light can we walk and act safely (Ex. 10:23; Job 12:24; Eccles. 2:13-14; Is. 42:16; 59:9-10). The law and the revelation which God graciously gave to Israel (Deut. 4:6-8, 32-40; 5:33; Wisd. 9:13-18), the wisdom found in them and identified with them are a light which guides pious people toward happiness, in God's grace and friendship (Ps. 119:105, 130; Prov. 6:23; Sir. 24:23, 30-34; cf. 45:17; 50:27-29; Bar. 1:1-4). On the other hand, the religious and moral blindness of the Israelites and of other nations is called darkness (Is. 42:16; 50:10; 60:2). In a few texts the light of law and revelation appears, lit in Israel as an eschatological gift meant also for the pagans (Is. 2:5; 42:4-6; 60:3), and it will be

[10] Whether in Prov. 20:27 the human conscience in this sense is called "a lamp of Yahweh" is very doubtful. Both the text and its explanation are very uncertain. The literal translation of the Hebrew is: "A lamp of Yahweh in the mind (literally: the breath) of man." Usually, with a slight correction of the original text, it is translated: "Yahweh beholds the mind of man." But this is not entirely satisfactory either.

carried throughout the world by Israel (Wisd. 18:4).

3. The light of life

Light is often connected with life, or life is represented as light. Certain expressions, in which the term "light" occurs in its real meaning, such as "to see the light" (Tob. 11:8: Tobias, cured from his blindness "looks on the light of days") or "to bring to the light" (Job 28:11; cf. 12:22) slowly change into a broader metaphoric meaning.

Human life is a journey from darkness, the womb (Ps. 139:11-16), toward darkness, the grave and the underworld (Job 10:19-22; 17:12-14; 18:18). Between these poles one makes his course "in the land of the living" (Ps. 27:13), i.e. among the people who live on earth. When a man is born he sees the light (Job 3:16; Bar. 3:20). When the twilight of the evening of his life sets in, dark days are approaching: the sun, the light, the moon and the stars begin to darken. When he dies his golden lamp breaks, his light goes out (Eccles. 11:8; 12:2, 6; Sir. 22:11). As long as Yahweh grants him the light (Job 3:20), i.e. as long as he keeps alive, he can see the sun and the light (Ps. 49:20; Eccles. 11:7).

A man's life can be so miserable that he does not appreciate this gift (Job 3:1-23; Jer. 20:14-18). He feels very unhappy. If his life threatens to come to an untimely end, he fears having incurred God's vengeance by his sins. "To live long in the land" is the remuneration which God promises to those who keep his law faithfully. How man exults if God in his mercy has kept him from the grave and allows him to "see the light" (Job 33:28) and to walk "in the light of life"[11] which God makes shine over him (Job 33:30; Ps. 56:14).

The light of life in this context evidently is something more than the light of earthly life. It denotes a life in well-being, as was the life of which Job in his misery keeps a nostalgic remembrance — "the day when God watched over me, when his lamp shone upon my head, and by his light I walked through darkness" (Job 29:2-3; 2 Sam. 22:29; Ps. 18:29).

4. The light of salvation and happiness

Prosperity, joy and salvation are often compared to warm and radiant light, while calamity, suffering and downfall are sometimes compared to destruction caused by fire (Is. 10:17; 30:27; 50:11; Joel 1:19-20; 2:3; Mal. 3:19); more often, in natural opposition, these are compared to cold and gloomy darkness

[11] In Job 33:28 we find "look at," "behold" in the meaning of, "see gladly," to rejoice in": this may be found in more places, (cf. Ps. 37:43). The translation of the *Psalterium Gallicanum: cum perierint peccatores, videbis* (you will see the destruction of the sinners) really means, as the *Psalterium Pianum* clarifies: *excidium peccatorum laetus videbis* (you will look on the destruction of the wicked). — In Ps. 56:14 and Job 33:30 the Hebrew word may be a noun "life," or an adjective used as a noun: "the living" (cf. "the land of the living"). It is therefore difficult to decide whether, along with the Septuagint in regard to the Psalms, and with Theodotion and some codices of the Septuagint in regard to Job, we must translate "the light of the living" or "the light of life." The latter translation seems more probable to us.

(Esther 8:16; Job 18:5-6; 30:26; Ps. 107:10-14; Prov.
13:19; Lam. 3:2; also Is. 43:11: "He will see the light,"
with the Septuagint and 1 Q Is a en Is b).

The happiness of the just man is like increasing
daylight (Judg. 5:31; Ps. 97:11; Prov. 4:18); the
strength of the light, moreover, seems directly pro-
portional to the happiness of God's people (Is. 30:26).
Not only is the happiness after a trial likened to the
morning which dispells darkness (Is. 8:20; 9:1; 58:
8-20); darkness and night are considered the appro-
priate time for vengeance and horror, just as morning
is the time for favor and salvation (Ps. 17:3, 15;
30:6; 46:6; Is. 17:14; 33:2; Zeph. 3:5 etc.).[12]

Yahweh, maker of light and darkness, creates both
salvation and doom. Whenever there is some decisive intervention of God, to show grace or to
bring punishment, light and darkness are frequently
mentioned. A tremendous upheaval in the cosmos
(an earthquake or an eclipse of the heavenly bodies)
is a compulsory accompaniment of the day of
Yahweh (Jer. 4:23; Ezek. 32:7-8; Joel 2:10-11; 3:3-4;
4:15-16; Amos 8:8-9). The day of Yahweh itself is
light for the just, but darkness for all who pay no
attention to God's will and law, and for those who,
like the children of Israel, are of opinion that the
day of the Lord could be light only for them (Is.
59:9; Jer. 13:16; Amos 5:18-20; Zeph. 1:14-18).

[12] Such an affinity and parallelism of nature and spiritual-
moral things is also characteristic of the description of man's
original condition, of the final fulfillment and, as we will
see below, of the day of Yahweh, and of moral good and evil.

The day of future restoration and messianic salvation, pre-eminently "the day of Yahweh," is especially a day of magnificent light (Is. 9:1-6; cf. Mt. 4:14-16; Is. 42:16; 62:1-2; Mic. 7:8-9). At that time of God's powerful salvation, his salutary victory, "the sun of righteousness" will rise, and his rays will bring salvation to all the just (Mal. 3:20; cf. Lk. 1:78: the word "righteousness," in Hebrew **sedaqah,** here means "saving victory, mighty salvation," as e.g. in Ps. 98:2; Is. 46:12 and 54:14). Then the light of God flows through the holy city and over the elect, so much so that they in their turn become resplendent like the sun (Is. 60:19; Bar. 5:1-9; Dan. 12:3). In these visions of the future the ideas of light and glory, expressing messianic salvation, often coincide. This is very understandable, since glory here still has the connotation of splendor of light.

5

SOURCES OF LIGHT

The source and cause of all these gifts of light mentioned in our last chapter is the generosity of the giver. We call a heavenly body or a lamp a light because it spreads light. In the same way we can give this name to the generosity of the benefactor from whom the blessings of spiritual life come.

1. Generosity as light

A metaphor which certainly influenced Zechariah in his visions of the sevenfold candelabrum (see above, chapter III) makes enchanting light (Ps. 8:4; Eccles. 11:7; Song 6:10; Sir. 43:1-10; Bar. 3:33-35) a synonym for generosity, bounty and grace. The same is true in the moving psalm of the Roman liturgy which the priest once prayed before ascending the altar (Ps. 43:3): "Oh send out thy light and thy truth; let them lead me, let them bring me to thy holy hill and to thy dwelling!" Light, linked with fidelity, is evidently divine favor or goodness. The pious poet, an exile, personifies them both; he asks God to send them as friendly messengers which may lead him from his abode of exile in the north (cf. Ps. 42:7), back toward the holy mount Zion (cf. 57:4, 11).

We find a similar metaphor in another psalm

(Ps. 36:10). Full of gratitude for the favors and joys
the faithful receive in the community of Israel and
in God's dwelling place (verse 9 "thy house"), the
psalmist prays: "For with thee is the fountain of
life, in thy light do we see light." This means: Because thou art propitious toward us ("in thy light")
we receive all happiness ("do we see light"). In
saying this he was not thinking only of the light of
wisdom, which was Israel's privilege and which is
also sometimes called "source of life" (Prov. 13:14;
16:22) but of all blessings, all happiness, all peace
which come forth from Yahweh, "the fountain of
living waters" (Jer. 2:13; 17:13). He was thinking
especially of the people's communing with their
infinitely amiable Lord, the source and sum of all
life and joy: "How gracious is thy steadfast love, O
God!" (Ps. 36:5, 7).

2. Man and God as light

The giver himself, because of his generosity and
his favors, sometimes is compared not only to the
light (cf. 2 Sam. 23:4), but, as the bearer of light,
he also is called a lamp. In this sense, in Ps. 112:4
the pious Israelite himself is called a light, for because of his virtue he is abundantly favored with
earthly goods and with these he helps his indigent
brethren: he is a light lit from the light of God.[13]

[13] This explanation of Ps. 112:4 is only probable. In the
Dutch *Canisius Bible* we find another explanation: the
generous Israelite here is not himself the light which dawns
upon the pious, but he is one of the pious people for whom
the light of God's blessings dawns. A third explanation is
possible: "Light rises in the darkness, for the upright, the

In a more exalted sense the Servant of Yahweh, who has been instructed by him, who undergoes such painful sufferings to expiate our iniquities, and who because of his obedience has been exalted and glorified, is the light of the nations. He cures the blind, releases captives from the darkness of their prisons; the salvation which comes from Yahweh radiates from him to the ends of the earth (Is. 42:6-7; 49:6; 50:4-6; 53:6, 10-12).

But above all God, the main source of all blessings, deserves to be called light. He is a light for those faithful to him, who find in him their protection and salvation (2 Sam. 22:29; Ps. 27:1). In Psalm 112:4, just mentioned, we find, according to another very probable explanation, the same.[14] God is also the light of Israel, but for the impious he is a fire (Is. 10:17). He is especially the light of the future new Jerusalem — so much so that it can do without the sun and the moon (Is. 60:1-3, 19-20; cf. Rev. 21:10-27). He is the light of the redeemed Zion, led by him from the darkness of misery toward the light (Mic. 7:7-9).

However, in the Old Testament God is never simply called light — an understandable attitude

Lord is gracious, merciful, and righteous." Yahweh himself then is the light. This explanation bases itself on the fact that the Hebrew terms which are translated here by gracious and merciful elsewhere in Holy Scripture refer only to God; (cf. Ps. 111:4; 145:8; Joel 2:13 etc.). This surely is an important indication; therefore we think this third explanation is no less probable than the first.

[14] Cf. note 13.

because of the pagan surroundings, where divine
honor was given to the heavenly bodies. The term
does not indicate his divine nature, but his disposition toward creatures. He is the light of his people
or of his servants because he grants them his favors.

This holds true where there can be no question
about the spiritual nature of the light, namely, the
personified Wisdom, which scrutinizes everything
and is the source of all that is good and beautiful;
it is called "the glow that radiates from eternal light"
(Wisd. 7:26; cf. Heb. 1:3). The name "the eternal
light" (cf. Is. 60:18-20), as is apparent from the context, does not here indicate God's nature but his
attitude toward creation: the power and splendor he
displays in it, the goodness and love he reveals in it.
All this is reflected in the divine wisdom described
here.

6

LIGHT OF RIGHTEOUSNESS
AND VIRTUE

As happiness and prosperity in the Old Testament are often compared to light and darkness, so also moral good and evil, in which they really have their cause, are thus described.

1. Light of virtue and darkness of sin

Light and darkness, prosperity and calamity, virtue and vice — living in accordance with or in opposition to God's law — these form many pairs of opposite notions (Prov. 7:9-10; Wisd. 17:1-5, 19-20; 18:1, 4; Is. 5:20).

Job described in vivid colors how murderers and adulterers seek darkness, how the godless hate and fear the light (Job 24:13-17). They fear the dawn, which expels them from the earth and robs them of their light, namely, of the darkness under cover of which they perpetrate their evil. Yahweh says to Job: "Have you commanded the morning since your days began, and caused the dawn to know its place, that it might take hold of the skirts of the earth, and the wicked be shaken out of it?" When dawn paints the earth in many colors, "from the

wicked their light is withheld, and their uplifted arm
is broken."[15]

In these texts light and darkness retain their original meaning. But the metaphoric meaning of virtue
and sin is even stronger. The just who obey God's
law walk in the light and the sunshine; the unjust
walk in darkness. On the day of judgment the unjust will realize, too late however, "that the ray of
justice never did enlighten them, never the true sun
shone" (Wisd. 5:6). The light of virtue i.e. the light
which comes forth from virtue or is virtue itself, here
signifies the wisdom of the just man. This wisdom,
given in God's law and revelation and put into
practice, is itself the virtuous life: i.e. the light of
virtue. The acknowledgment of the godless here
does not mean that moral obligations were unknown
to them but, as the author says, they "forsake the
paths of uprighteousness" — in other words, they
do not heed God's law (cf. Prov. 2:13-15).

2. Children of light and children of darkness

In the documents of Qumrân,[16] found in 1947,

---

[15] For this translation of Job 38:12-15 see a. o. Le Livre
de Job 2, in the *Bible de Jérusalem,* Paris 1957, p. 153, or
the *Bible of the Dutch Bible Society.* The devious translation of our *Canisius Bible* looks less felicitous.

[16] About these documents see J. van der Ploeg, *Vondsten
in de Woestijn van Juda,* Utrecht 1957; especially pp. 89-97
and 165-192; from the same author: "Handschriften der
Woestijn van Juda," in *Bijbels Woordenboek 2,* Aanhangsel
I, c. 1957-1970 (cf. note 3); R. Mayer and J. Reuss, *Dodezee-
rollen en Bijbel* (Dutch translation: A. van den Born),
Roermond en Maaseik 1960, especially pp. 66-78 and 146-148;
155-162.

especially in 1 QS III. 13-IV. 20, and in other Jewish documents, light and darkness signify two opposite worlds of moral good and evil, of the just and the unjust, who are called children of light and children of darkness. Children of light indicates members of the community to which the author belongs. The two realms of good and evil are hostile toward one another. In their mutual struggle one is led by the prince of light and the other by the angel of darkness, of perdition, of evil.

Such a viewpoint is familiar to us. It is true that we do not find this in a developed form in the Old Testament; but it is an extension of the ideas we find there. According to the accepted opinion of the time (as we saw in our first chapter) light and darkness are two independent entities, each with its own territory. Struggle between the unjust and the just is a topic repeated often in Scripture. It is quite normal in Semitic languages that many relationships are expressed in familiar terms: thus in Arabic the cock is "the father of awakening" and the traveller "the son of the road." Though some expressions in the Qumrân texts are obscure and equivocal, quite probably even according to these texts a man does not belong to the children of light or to the children of darkness as a result of blind fate or a fatal destiny, but as a consequence of a personal free choice of his own will. Even the idea that an angel of darkness rules over the realm of darkness has its roots in the Old Testament. The Old Testament speaks about a being hostile to God, whom the Hebrew

Bible calls **sàtàn,** (adversary, accuser) and the Greek
Bible **diabolos** (devil, calumniator). This being tries
to damage God's domination by seducing his creatures, starting from the first human couple, to sin
(Gen. 3; Wisd. 2:24-25).

Of course it is possible, because of long contact
between Jews and Persians, that Persian thought,
with its dual world of evil and good, contributed to
the fact that the Jews came to give more exact
formulation to some ideas already found in the Old
Testament. There need not have been any direct
dependence as regard the doctrine. Of one detail
however we can trace no indication in Scripture,
namely, that against the angel of darkness there
stands an angel of light, who is the leader of the
powers of light. It does not seem presumptuous or
unfounded to think here of a direct or indirect influence from Persian thought. The Persians accept
two principles, which from the beginning stand next
to one another and fight one another, until at the
end of time the principle of good will be victorious.

There remains however a radical difference. In
the Jewish writings the prince of light and the angel
of darkness are, in their existence and in their actions,
dependent upon God who created everything. He
it is who on the day of his visitation or of the
fulfillment will stop the combat, by granting victory
to the good.

PART II

THE NEW TESTAMENT ON LIGHT

Light, glory and like terms, as spiritual values, are used in the New Testament in about the same way as they were in the Old. The language in the later writings of the Old Testament and in the New is often a peculiar mixture of old texts which, in whole or in part, are sometimes quoted from disparate biblical contexts. A single word or even an allusion is expected to remind the reader of well known Bible texts. Such references may recall seemingly contradictory prophecies, as e.g. the prophecies about Christ's divine exaltation and his human form of the Servant: these two aspects indeed are realized in the one person of the Redeemer. As an example of this, one might read John 12:37-41, a passage about which we shall speak later.

Instructed as they were by their Master, the disciples considered Christ and his mission to be the fulfillment of the prophecies of Holy Scripture concerning the revelation of God's light and glory in the far future, the great day of Yahweh; the Servant of Yahweh and his painful sufferings; the enigmatic Son of Man and his eternal dominion over the world.

To correctly understand the New Testament texts in this matter it is necessary to keep one thing in

mind: in the Old Testament God's decisive intervention at the end of time is described as one single
event. The course of Jesus' earthly life and his
preaching however taught his followers that this
ought not to be understood as an event of one day
or hour; it is a unity of events which constituted
God's economy of salvation developing itself in
several successive moments. That is why in quoting
the Old Testament they sometimes have in mind one
or several moments in this development, and at
another time the whole plan.

Light and glory as ingredients of the messianic
happiness often coincide. But because of the very
particular meaning of the word "glory" in biblical
language it is better to consider them separately.

7

JESUS CROWNED WITH GLORY
BECAUSE OF HIS PASSION

In the New Testament the Greek word **doxa** (glory), together with the derived verb **doxázein** (glorify), frequently has the meaning of splendor (Acts 22:11; 1 Cor. 15:40-41; Rev. 18:1); it also has several other meanings.

In allusions to the Old Testament, which may be more or less clear, **doxa** is the glory of Yahweh, as we have already seen (Acts 7:2; cf. Ps. 29:3; Rom. 9:4; 2 Cor. 3:7-13; cf. Ex. 34:29-35; Heb. 9:5; Rev. 15:8). More frequently, in a more spiritualized sense, it is the splendid revelation of God's perfections or of God himself in the display of his exalted power and majesty, his wisdom or goodness (Jn. 11:40; Acts 7:55; Rom. 1:23; cf. Ps. 106:20 and Jer. 2:11; Rom. 6:4; 9:23; Eph. 1:6, 12, 14; 3:16; Col. 1:11; 1 Thess. 2:12; Heb. 1:3; Jude 24). In some of these texts allusions are made to Christ and his mission and the glory in and around the Lord Jesus is outlined in Yahweh's glory.

1. The glory of the Son of Man
The glory which the prophets foretold would one day rise in splendor over the world is the glory which

belongs to Christ. On the day of Yahweh, the day of
God's tremendous judgment, a day of light for the
just and of darkness for the godless — on that day
the Son of Man will come with his angels (cf. Is. 6:2-3;
Ezek. 10:4); he will come in the glory of his Father
(Mt. 16:27; Mk. 8:38), in his own glory (Mt. 25:31;
2 Thess. 1:9-10), in the glory which is at the same
time his and his Father's (Lk. 9:26) in order to requite
everyone according to his merits.

The nations will see him coming on the clouds
of heaven, with great power and majesty (Mt. 24:30;
cf. 19:28; Mk. 13:26; Lk. 21:27).

These texts refer to the famous vision of Daniel
(7:9-27). But while the first group has the Son of Man
coming at the end of time to judge the world, the
second group has him establish an everlasting reign
among men. His coming, throughout the ages, is
one coherent scheme. In this scheme one summit
is the end of the old economy at the destruction of
Jerusalem; this in turn is at the same time the prefiguration of and the prelude to the other summit,
the end of the world and the general judgment.

2. The glorification of the Servant of Yahweh

By his resurrection and ascension Christ entered
into his glory (Lk. 24:26; Phil. 3:21; 1 Tim. 3:16;
Heb. 2:7, 9; 1 Pet. 1:11, 21; cf. Acts 3:13). When
the prophecies had not yet been fulfilled in Jesus,
it was difficult to see how he could be the Son of
Man coming on the clouds, in whom God's glory
and eternal dominion over the entire world would

be realized. When the Servant of Yahweh was so much disfigured and maltreated that his appearance was no longer human, it is difficult to understand the statement. "Who has believed what we have heard? And to whom is the arm of Yahweh revealed?" (Is. 53:1). But the prophet also announced that he would be exalted and glorified, and God in him, or (as the Septuagint, usually used by the authors of the New Testament says) that he would be highly exalted, and God in him (Is. 49:3, 5; 52:13).

When Jesus of Nazareth had risen and had seated himself at the right hand of the Most High, it became evident that all things fell into place according to the divine plan: he is "crowned with glory and honor because of the suffering of death" (Heb. 2:9). Preachers of the new faith often refer to the prophets and announce that God has raised his Servant from the dead, that he has glorified him (Acts 3:13, 16) and has appointed him to be Lord and judge of the living and the dead (Acts 2:36; 10:42; 13:30-41; Rom. 1:4; Phil. 2:8-11; Heb. 1:2-4). The Man of sorrows, bruised for the iniquities of men, was vested with glory because of his intense suffering (Is. 53:10-11); he was equipped to vanquish in and through his Church all powers of darkness, to make God's glory radiate over all the earth, to lead all men of good will into his glorious eternal kingdom (1 Thess. 1:10; 2 Thess. 1:9-10).

Thus it was shown to the seer of Patmos in his grandiose visions: the Son of Man who had died but

now lives in all eternity, stands in the midst of the
seven golden lampstands; here is the image of God's
constant vigilance over the Church and of the
service which the Church is bound to render him
in sincere piety and unwearying faith (Rev. 1:12, 20;
2:1-5; 5:6; 11:3-13; cf. Zech. 3:1-5, 10-14); the slain
Lamb is victorious in his death, and is therefore
allowed to read God's plans for the world into the
book which is sealed with seven seals, and will put
these plans into execution (Rev. 5:6-13; 14:1-5; 17:14);
on the great day of Yahweh throughout the ages up
to the last judgment he will celebrate his victory
(Rev. 19:11-21; 8) and he will make the splendor of
God's glory shine over the new Jerusalem, his
Church (Rev. 21:9-22; 5).

3. The glory of the transfiguration of the Lord

Some time before the disciples' faith in Jesus'
messianic dignity would be put to a severe test by
his shameful death upon the cross, he fortified this
faith by showing them how the prophecies concerning
the Servant of Yahweh could harmonize with those
about the Son of Man who received glory and eternal
kingship from God. In the transfiguration of the
Lord (Mt. 17:1-9; Mk. 9:2-10; Lk. 9:28-36; 1 Pet.
1:16-19; cf. 1:3) they foresaw the glory which belongs to him and would come to him after he had
travelled the road of his passion in Jerusalem to
the very end. Among the evangelists only Luke
mentions the glory and ascribes it to Jesus. But in
the other two we find mention of the resplendent
cloud out of which God's voice resounds. This cloud

evidently is Yahweh's glory which envelops Jesus, Moses and Eliah. In his second letter Peter considers the apparition of Yahweh's glory on Sinai (Ex. 24:16-17) as a preview of Jesus' transfiguration on the holy mountain. He says that the Majestic Glory, God, revealed himself in this glory and made his voice heard in order to give honor to Jesus. According to the four witnesses, the event on the mountain showed the disciples the power and majesty with which the glorified Redeemer would come to establish his kingdom (Mt. 16:28; Mk. 9:1; Lk. 9:27; 2 Pet. 1:11, 16).

This visible revelation of Jesus' glory was a single and passing phenomenon in his earthly career. It was reserved for a few privileged disciples, who would testify about it after his resurrection. We do perceive a brief momentary flash of God's glory when Jesus is born (Lk.2:9), but this shone around the shepherds, not above the crib. Simeon praises the Lord when he holds the child Jesus in his arms, because he has been allowed to see the salvation, "a light for revelation to the Gentiles and for glory to thy people Israel" (Lk. 2:30-32). But the light and the glory remain invisible. Simeon sees only with the eyes of the mind and as a prophet, that in this child will be realized what was written by Isaiah about the Servant of Yahweh, "a covenant to the people, a light to the nations" (Is. 42:6; 49:6); in him, too, is the mighty dawn of Yahweh's glory over the true Israel of the future (Is. 60:1-3) in the new and eternal covenant (cf. Ex. 24:7-8, 16-17).

4. The glorified Lord in the doxologies

The word **doxa** is often found in doxologies or in
connection with them; they are more or less solemn
liturgical formulas in which praise is given to God
or, occasionally, to the Lord Jesus.[17] Frequently, in
the original language, they have no verb: "to him
the **doxa**" or some similar expression is used. The
question is whether these are to be understood as
a wish or a prayer: "To him be the **doxa**," or as a
declaration, as in Pet. 4:11, where the verb expresses
a statement or an acknowledgment: "To him is the
doxa; he possesses it." This is a difficult question.
Some scholars feel that these words in the New
Testament are always an acknowledgment. According to others they express a wish. We will probably
have to judge each in its own context. In order to
find the meaning of the word **doxa** in the doxologies
we cannot invariably take the standpoint that it is
always a prayer, nor that it is always an acknowledgment.

The word often means homage, honor, esteem
which befalls someone or which he seeks (Lk. 14:10;
17:15, 18). Thus the adversaries of Jesus try to gain
doxa with the people, while he himself in his entire
human existence gives **doxa** to the Father (Jn. 5:44;
7:18; 12:43; 17:4); after rising and being glorified, he
will do this in an even more exalted manner (Jn.

[17] Cf. A. van den Born, "Doxologie," in *Bijbels Woordenboek 2*, c. 379-380. We need to pay attention here only to
doxologies in a strict sense, i.e. those in which the word
doxa occurs.

14:13; 15:8; 17:1). With the meaning of something (homage, honor) given by man to God or to Christ, or given by Christ as man to the Father, **doxa** surely may be the object of a prayer; but it is also a joyful acknowledgment of the fact that such honor as is due to him is indeed being given.

The word may however also signify a divine reality. Whenever this is the case, we cannot at once conclude that the **doxa** may only be the object of an acknowledgment. Indeed, when it expresses an attribute of the deity or an event which can only come about through God — something in which created nature cannot at all be actively involved — we surely can only acknowledge it, not wish for it. But we can still utter a wish **about** it. Thus Jesus teaches us to pray: Our Father, thy name — thy exalted majesty — be hallowed; thy kingdom come (Mt. 6:9-10); he too prays: Father, glorify thy name (Jn. 12:28).

With many doxologies the great difficulty is to decide whether the **doxa** must be understood as homage of creature to God, or as a possession or an action of God. This is not only the case when the word stands alone, but also when it is used together with other words. It is remarkable that in several doxologies terms are found which have both meanings; Rev. 7:12, mentions along with the **doxa** on the one hand wisdom, power and strength, and on the other hand praise, thanks and homage.

Doxologies which indicate homage without a doubt are more numerous. In most of them this

homage is given to God, almost always because of
the salvation which appeared in Christ. In some
however the homage is given to the Lord Jesus,
always because of salvation received through him
(Heb. 13:21; Rev. 5:12-13).

But there are others in which the word **doxa**
indicates a reality which belongs to God (Jude 25;
probably also Rev. 7:12 and 19:1) or to Christ (1 Pet.
4:11; Rev. 1:6). In this context the topic is always
Jesus' work of redemption: the **doxa** is the power
and majesty of God as it revealed itself in the victory
of Christ over sin and death; or it is the glory sur-
rounding the risen Redeemer.[18]

Those addressed to Christ therefore concern only
the glory which we mentioned before, namely, the
glory which Jesus received at his resurrection. They
do not concern, at least not directly, the glory which
he possesses as the Son of God in his pre-existence.

[18] This undoubtedly is also the case in the great doxology
taken from the Greek into the Latin liturgy: *Gloria in
excelsis Deo,* and the reason: *Gratias agimus Tibi propter
magnam gloriam tuam.* The great glory for which we thank
the holy Trinity is not the eternal glory of God, but the
power and majesty which the divine persons reveal in the
creation and the redemption.

8

THE GLORY OF THE SON IN JOHN

It is necessary to devote a special chapter to the doctrine about the glory of Jesus in the fourth gospel.[19] From the way John speaks — or also keeps silent, as when he does not mention the Transfiguration of the Lord — some critics conclude that the glory which manifested itself at the resurrection of Jesus' body was of no importance to the evangelist; only the glory of the Son of God which he possesses by nature and which he displays from the beginning in all his works, they say, are of interest to John. We hope to make it sufficiently clear that such contrast between John and the other evangelists does not exist. It is certain that beside the momentary glory radiating from Jesus' resurrection, John is aware of a glory inaccessible to the senses and existing in reality long before the resurrection of Jesus.

1. The glory of the resurrection

John repeatedly speaks about the glory which encompassed Jesus at his resurrection (Jn. 7:39; 12:16,

---

[19] An important essay about Word, light, life and glory in John is Jacques Dupont's *Essai sur la Christologie de saint Jean,* Bruges 1951. Also W. Grossouw, *Het christendom van Johannes,* 's-Hertogenbosch 1942.

23; 13:31-32; 17:1-5). If at times we notice elsewhere
some contrast between the shame of the death on
the cross and the glory which followed it (Acts 2:36;
3:13; 1 Pet. 1:11), this is because John puts special
stress on the connection between suffering and
glorification. He connects the two kinds of **doxa**
which we know: one, the homage which people and
especially Jesus give to God in their words and works;
the other, the glory which God grants because of this.

He especially emphasizes this connection in the
death and resurrection of Christ. Christ is not only
glorified because of his cruel suffering, as was
prophesied about the Servant of Yahweh and as
we read in several places in the New Testament;
his suffering also constitutes his supreme homage to
the Father, and his ascent toward the glory which
the Father grants him. His sufferings and his glorification are seen as one and the same thing. The
hour of his passion is also the hour of his glorification (Jn. 12:23-28; 13:1; 17:1); at the moment Judas
leaves the room of the Last Supper, Jesus begins
his movement toward being sacrificed and glorified
(Jn. 13:31-32). In the plan which the Father stipulated
and which was accepted in obedience by the Son
(Jn. 10:17-18; 14:31), the glorification develops from
the passion; it is at the same time its crowning.

Although some writers say so, it is not exactly
true that for John the passion is already the glorification: Jesus' passion in John's description loses
none of its humiliation and horror. But it is true
that, for John, glorification is seminally present in

the passion. For this glorification Jesus prays a few hours before his death (Jn. 7:1, 4-5): "Father, . . . glorify thy Son." When he adds: "that the Son may glorify thee," he expresses in other words what the other evangelists described as the coming in glory of the Son of Man to establish the kingdom of God. He does the same when he says that the Father will be glorified in and through the disciples (Jn. 14:13; 15:8; 21:19), or that the glorification of the Father through the Son is at the same time the glorification of the Son through the Spirit of truth (Jn. 16:12-15).

2. Glory which precedes the resurrection

This glorification as the crowning of the passion is also surely intended when John concludes the story of Jesus' preaching and prepares the story of his passion and resurrection (12:37-41) by texts referring to Isaiah. Mention of the Servant of Yahweh (Is. 53:1), of the unbelief of Israel (Is. 6:9-10), and an unmistakable allusion to a third about Yahweh's glory (Is. 6:1-4) also present to us the unbelief of the Jews at the same time. Jesus' passion and glorification are the inscrutable counsel of God, in which all things are held together. "The glory which Isaiah has seen" in this context must be the glory which Jesus received at his resurrection. The prophet saw this, not as if it existed at the time of Isaiah, but as prophets in a vision see things which still lie in a far future (cf. Jn. 8:56).

However, the words of the evangelist suppose a glory of Jesus which existed before his resurrection: "Though he (Jesus) had done so many signs before them, yet they did not believe in him" (Jn. 12:37). This is the same as "they have not believed in his glory." Miracles for John are signs of Jesus' glory (Jn. 2:11; 11:4, 40). This is hidden here; it cannot be seen with the eyes, but reveals itself to the faith of those who can understand the significance of the miracles.

The prologue of his gospel speaks about this glory which existed before Jesus' resurrection: "Full of grace and truth; we have beheld his glory, glory as of the only Son from the Father" (Jn. 1:14). The other authors of the New Testament consider Jesus' resurrection and his coming with great majesty to be the fulfillment of what the prophets foretold about the eschatological time. As we have seen, John too knows about this glory. But to him this eschatological glory is the splendid revelation of that glory which was due, and already given, to the Redeemer when first he came into this world. Even our own resurrection from the dead, as participation in Jesus' resurrection, the final judgment, the gift of eternal life — all these and others which belong to the glory of the Lord at his second advent, John considers present as soon as Jesus appears and begins his public life. But just like the glory of the Lord up to the time of his resurrection, all these eschato- logical realities are, for the time being, discernible only to the eye of faith. Whatever is found in the prophets concerning the appearance of Yahweh's glory in the far future and whatever is found in the Wisdom books (which as we shall see had a great influence on John) concerning the divine wisdom residing in God's holy temple in Jerusalem (Sir. 24:7-22) — all this John sees as realized in the incarnation of the divine Word and in his residence among men. As soon as the Word is made man, the glory of Yahweh takes possession of his sanctuary in the midst of his chosen people in a much more perfect way than before; God's wisdom takes up its residence in the holy temple (Jn. 2:21). The glory which the disciples beheld (Jn. 1:14) is the glory of God's incarnate Son. This undoubtedly is true of the radiant glory of his resurrection and, for a moment, the glory of his transfiguration.[20] But it is true as well for the glory which as yet remained hidden and was visible only to those who believe in the miracles of Jesus.

The Father has already glorified his Son, especially through the works and miracles which he gave him to do (Jn. 3:35; 5:20-36; 10:25, 37-38; 14:10-11, 24) and through the disciples he gave him, in order that they also would receive glory, resurrection and eternal life from him (Jn. 6:37-40, 44-47; 17:6-10); and the Son glorified the Father before he rose from the dead (Jn. 7:18; 8:50, 54; 11:4, 40; 12:28; 17:4).

But this preceding glory in no way diminishes the importance of the glorification on the occasion of

---

[20] Possibly the words "glory as of the only Son from the Father" (Jn. 1:14) allude to the story of the transfiguration as it is found in Lk. 9:32, 33. The traditions as found in Luke and John are often interrelated.

the resurrection. Very pointedly and insistently John
refers to this as the decisive moment in the history
of redemption. After Jesus has been glorified, he
will glorify the Father in a manner even more exalted
than he did before. Then in answer to the prayers
of the disciples the highest gifts are given; then the
Spirit of truth comes and pours his consolation and
strength into their hearts; he glorifies Jesus and
testifies about him in and through his disciples, in
and through their mutual love, in and through the
productivity of their lives, their miraculous activity
(Jn. 7:39; 14:12-14; 15:7-10, 26-27; 16:7-15; 17:1, 26;
1 Jn. 5:6-8). Then finally the apostles, through the
light of the Spirit, will understand the mystery of
Jesus' person, the meaning of the Scriptures, and the
deep significance of what happened to Jesus, and
his actions (Jn. 2.22; 12:16; 13:7; 14, 26; 16:13; 20:9).
In brief, the hidden glory which preceded Jesus'
resurrection was revealed to John in a clear way
only at the glorious resurrection of Jesus.

3. Jesus' glory with God before the world existed

In the texts seen so far, the glory ascribed to
Christ is never directly the eternal majesty and
perfection of God's Word. Of course, the sacred
authors, especially Paul and John, very clearly suppose this as the deeper ground of Jesus' glory. But
what they speak of is the glory of the Messiah, the
incarnate Son; they speak of the mission he came
to fulfill as Lord and supreme Judge appointed by
God. Even the title "Son of God" does not prove
that the glory must be differently understood: this

name more than once is the equivalent of Messiah
or Christ (cf. Jn. 1:49; 3:14-16; 5:25-27; 11:27); in any
case, it is not used exclusively for the Son in his
eternal pre-existence.

It is true that Jesus at times is given the title
"Lord of glory" (1 Cor. 2:8 and probably Jas. 2:1,
though this text may be explained differently), a
name which in the literature of Judaism indicates
God himself (Hen. 22:14; 27:3, 5; cf. "the God of
glory" Ps. 29:3; Acts 7:1). But evidently the Lord
of glory here is the incarnate Son, who possesses the
glory (Jas.) or to whom it rightly belongs (1 Cor.)
because of his mission of salvation.

There are only two texts in John (Jn. 17:5, 24)
which, according to many scholars, refer to the
glory of the Son in his eternal pre-existence. This
opinion still looks probable to us.[21] But it is possible
that the evangelist, following the New Testament
method of speaking refers to the glory which is the
constant topic in the high-priestly prayer of Jesus:
the resurrection, the ascension, the pouring out of
the Holy Spirit. We prefer this opinion. When
Jesus prays: "And now, Father, glorify thou me in
thy own presence with the glory which I had with

[21] Cf. L. Sibum, "Jezus' Gebed om de Eenheid van al de
zijnen" (Jo. XVII), in *Het Christelijk Oosten en Hereeniging*
I (1949) pp. 205-228, where we explained this opinion. In
the same way, but in a more resolute manner, H. van den
Bussche, *Jezus' Woorden van het Afscheidsmaal*, Tielt en
Den Haag 1955; he rejects the other opinion explicitly
(p. 173).

thee before the world was made" (Jn. 17:5), this may
signify "give me the glory which you had destined
for me from all eternity."[22]

This is also what we quite naturally read in the
second text (Jn. 17:24). The Redeemer, who in his
prayer speaks as if his earthly life had already been
finished and as if he had already been glorified
(Jn. 17:4, 6, 11-12) says: "Father, I desire that they
also, whom thou hast given me, may be with me
where I am, to behold my glory which thou hast
given me in thy love for me before the foundation
of the world." He does not say that the glory had
been given him before the creation of the world, but
that God in his eternal love destined this glory for
him (cf. 1 Pet. 1:20) — the glory which radiates in
his resurrection and which henceforth will be eter-
nally his.

---

[22] There are variant readings which point out that in the
original text the words "I had" were lacking and that it
therefore reads: "the glory which (was) with thee." In
this case this explanation would be preferable.

9

PARTICIPANTS OF JESUS' GLORY

In the last-quoted text of John (Jn. 17:24) we note an idea also found elsewhere: that the glory of Jesus is not restricted to him alone; it flows over to those whom he has chosen.

1. Glory in the future and at present

The faithful disciples of Jesus expect that at the end of time God "the Father (giver) of glory" (Eph. 1:17) will also give them the glory, just as he gave it to Jesus (1 Pet. 1:21); they expect that the glorified Jesus himself will make them participants of his glory (Jn. 17:24; Rom. 2:7, 10; 5:2; 8:18-21; 9:23; 1 Cor. 14:43; 2 Cor. 4:17; Eph. 1:18; Phil. 3:20-21; 1 Thess. 1:12; 2 Tim. 2:10; 1 Pet. 4:13-14; cf. Rom. 8:11; 1 Pet. 5:1, 4, 10).

But some texts mention a participation in God's glory or in Christ's glorification as already present in this earthly life. When Paul teaches that both Jews and gentiles are justified only through the faith in Jesus, he writes: "For there is no distinction; since all have sinned and fall short of the glory of God" (Rom. 3:23). According to many scholars this means that because of their evil ways they cannot find any appreciation or favorable judgment with God. It would be better to say that the apostle is thinking here of the glory of God in which the Jews rejoiced (Rom. 9:4), which according to Ezekiel, withdraws from a sinful people only to return in the messianic time. This glory therefore, through Christ, becomes the possession of all who are justified through faith in him, and as soon as they are justified.

The apostle knows that there are some who consider him lacking in splendor of words and wisdom. He reminds them that his doctrine (the economy of salvation which was established from all eternity and realized in the crucified Christ) constitutes an exalted wisdom, at least for those who have come to fruition in a Christian life. It is "a wisdom which God decreed before the ages for our glorification" (Rom. 2:7). "Our glorification" here is evidently not our future glory, but the resplendent revelation, in and through the Church, of the manifold wisdom of God (Eph. 3:10-12) the whole treasures of graces which Christ communicates to the members of his body, the Church (Eph. 1:22; Col. 1:18-23). Our resurrection from the dead is its glorious crowning.

In other texts the glory radiating from the face of Moses after an interview with Yahweh (Ex. 34:29-35) is used to prove the excellence of Christ's economy of salvation. In Hebrews (3:2-3) the **doxa** given to Moses must be understood as the honor or the dignity which Moses receives. But in the second letter to the Corinthians the glory of Moses' face is especially mentioned and it is an important fea-

ture in his argumentation. The old covenant certainly was attended with glory: it radiated from
Moses' face, so much so that the sons of Israel could
not stand the splendor of it. But what is this transient
glory of the provisionary covenant in comparison
with that of the new and lasting covenant? In comparison, it is like nothing (2 Cor. 3:7-11). Paul continues: When Moses spoke to the Israelites, he
covered the radiance of his face with a veil; but
when he appeared before Yahweh, he removed this
veil. In this way all of us who believe are standing
unveiled before the Lord Jesus: we reflect the glory
of God which shines in his face and thus, by the influence of the gloriously radiating Christ, we are
recreated unto an ever increasing likeness to him.
Literally: "We . . . are being changed into his likeness from one degree of glory to another" (2 Cor.
3:18). This reaches us in the gospel of Christ's glory,
which the apostles carry out as a divine light over
the world (2 Cor. 3:12-18; 4:1-6). This, increasing
continually in those who are baptized and changing
them constantly (from one degree of glory to another)
into the likeness of the glorified Christ, evidently
is the new life unto which Christ has risen. In this
they grow until finally their bodies too are made
similar to his glorified body (Rom. 6:4-11; 8:29-30).

Sometimes Paul (Eph. 2:6; Col. 2:12) describes the
communion of Christians with the crucified and risen
Redeemer as so intimate that they appear as participants in his death and glorified heavenly existence.
They have died with Christ and in him they have

been raised from the dead and are seated in heavenly glory. He exhorts them: "If then you have been raised with Christ, seek the things that are above, where Christ is, seated at the right hand of God . . . For you have died, and your life is hid with Christ in God. When Christ who is our life appears, then you also will appear with him in glory" (Col. 3:1, 3-4). By faith and baptism the faithful share even in this world in a spiritual way in the glory of the risen Christ. The glorious resurrection on Christ's second advent will make apparent the glory which they possess in a hidden way on earth.

2. Glory which creates unity

From the texts of Paul, just quoted, it is evident that according to his vision the glory which radiates in the risen Redeemer is not a quality of his body only. The fourth gospel agrees with him in this, as it does in the doctrine that Christians here and hereafter share in the glory of the risen Christ. On the eve of his passion we hear Jesus pray for all those who through the word of the apostles will believe in him — all who within the communion of the Church conform themselves to the reason, heart and will of Jesus. Continuously speaking as if he had already been taken up into the heavenly glory he says to the Father: "The glory which thou hast given me I have given to them, that they may be one" even as we are one" (Jn. 17:22). The glory given to Jesus at the moment of his incarnation usually remained hidden during his earthly existence. But it radiates in an unprecedented way as soon as he was united with his Father. Jesus made his followers participants of this glory. But in them also it remains hidden: they possess it in the darkness of their faith. Only when they will be where he himself resides, glorified with his Father, will they see this glory resplendent in him and in themselves (Jn. 17:24; cf. 5:28-29; 6:39, 40, 54, 62).

Jesus had also told them how this glory, which on earth can be seen only through faith is truly a reality within them, how potently it is active in them and about them. As in the Old Testament so also here the glory is the heart and source of unity; but it is a unity so intimate and holy that it has its roots in the unity of the Father and the incarnate Son, and participates in it; it is a unity so wonderful that it will be proof of the divine mission of Jesus to the unbelieving world: "The glory which thou hast given me I have given to them, that they may be one even as we are one, I in them and thou in me, that they may become perfectly one, so that the world may know that thou hast sent me and hast loved them even as thou hast loved me" (Jn. 17:22-23).

The evangelist himself tries to give some description of this love of God for the Church of Christ, when at the beginning of his book he says that he who is the true light has given those who will believe in his name the power to become children of God. How will they be children of God? Evidently by sharing in the glory which he as the only begotten Son received from the Father: "fullness . . . of grace and truth," from which all have in turn received (Jn. 1:12-18).

This leads us to the second section of our considerations of the question: What does the New Testament say about light?

10

LIGHT IN THE PROPER

SPHERE OF THE NEW TESTAMENT

It is a remarkable feature of New Testament doctrine that on the one hand it is so closely connected with the teaching of the Old Testament, while on the other hand it displays so many new and hitherto unknown treasures. This will be evident from numerous texts where the term "light" occurs in comparisons and metaphors.

1. Comparison between the New and Old Testament

"Light" occurs in the New Testament in its normal meaning of brightness (Mt. 10:27; Lk. 8:16; Jn. 11:10; cf. 5:36; Rev. 18:23; 22:5) or source of light (Mk. 14:45; Jn. 11:9; Acts 16:29; Jas. 1:17).

New Testament authors like those of the Old Testament think that light, like glory, surrounds God or those who reside with him in the heavenly abode: the angels and, after his glorification, the Redeemer (2 Cor. 11:14; 1 Tim. 6:16). Whenever a visibly discernible event is mentioned, the light which accompanies it is meant as something visible; at the transfiguration of Jesus (Mt. 17:2; cf. 17:5: "a bright cloud"), at Paul's conversion where the light surrounds

the glorified Christ (Acts 9:3; 22:6-11; 26:13), or at
the apparition of an angel (Acts 12:7; cf. Rev. 18:1).

In the New Testament light no longer means a
long and happy life on earth, promised in the old
books of the Bible to those who kept the law. In
the New Testament it means higher things, coming
from the same divine benignity and love which
prophets and psalmists pointed out over and above
those earthly blessings, and praised as an infinitely
greater gift and as an infinitely more enviable light.
The conviction, gained by experience, that virtue
is not always a guarantee of temporal prosperity
was already expressed in the Old Testament, where
the term **anâwim** ("the poor, the lowly") is used to
indicate the pious people. We meet this for the first
time, scholars think, around the year 635 B.C. in
Zephaniah 2:3; 3:11-13. Later writings teach explicitly that God has something better in store for
his friends than a blessed old age and a numerous
progeny (Wisd. 1:6; 5:15). The New Testament
adds that higher things come to the elect in Christ.

2. The New Testament compared with Judaism

With regard to light and darkness in matters of
religion and morals, the New Testament shows a
certain similarity to the ideas we met (chapter VI)
in Judaism, especially in the circles of Qumrân. But
this similarity concerns precisely those ideas which
we find in the Old Testament. Indeed the New
Testament too mentions a world of the children of
light and one of the children of darkness. More
clearly than other Jewish writing however it teaches

that a man becomes a child of light or of darkness
in consequence of a freely made choice, in which he
accepts or rejects a loving offer of God (Mt. 7:24-27;
Jn. 3:19-21; 5:39-40; 6:66-67; 12:34-36). Moreover it
teaches that God's love reveals itself in Christ and
embraces all men.

Just as these writings mention an angel of darkness
who is the leader in the realm of darkness, so there
is also one in the New Testament. Here he is called
devil, satan, lord of this world. Jesus' countrymen
call him the prince of devils (Mt. 9:34; 25:41; Jn.
12:31; Acts 26:18). Perhaps once he is also called
Beliar (Belial) (2 Cor. 6:15), as occurs repeatedly in
the literature of Qumrân. But Paul may wish to
indicate the antichrist by this name.

In the New Testament we do not find a created
prince or leader of the realm of light. When Paul
says (2 Cor. 11:14) that "even satan disguises himself
as an angel of light," he is thinking of an angel who
hails from the sphere of the light in which God
dwells with many angels. He is not a leader of the
powers or of the children of light. Only the divine
Ruler has authority over the light in this religious
and moral sense.

11

SHINING STARS IN A DARK WORLD

The texts of the New Testament in which light and like terms are used in matters of religion and morals are rather numerous. It is remarkable that the light of virtue is always considered in connection with Christ.

1. Called from darkness unto light

Whenever the Master uses light to illustrate some lesson or exhortation by a simple comparison, the word retains its own meaning, yet is used to illustrate a higher doctrine: e.g. the duty of the apostles to preach openly and unfearingly, manifesting the gospel which hitherto had to remain hidden (Mk. 4:21-22; Lk. 8:16-17; cf. Mt. 10:27) or the duty of his followers to be open and honest, and not to envelop themselves in pharisaic hypocrisy (Lk. 12:2-3; cf. Mt. 10:25-26).

We find Job's idea about a kind of kinship between darkness and sin, and about sinners who hate the light and love darkness (Job 24:13-17; 28:12-15) returning in the New Testament with the same intermingling of the literary and the metaphoric (Jn. 3:19-21; Rom. 13:11-13; Eph. 5:8-14; 1 Thess. 5:7-8). We see this in a very striking way in the beginning

of the drama of the passion, when Judas leaves the
room in order to carry out his plan of treason: "And it
was night" (Jn. 13:30; cf. Lk. 22:53).

Later books of the Bible and Judaic writings do
not say that only pagans are living in darkness. In
the New Testament Paul very expressly teaches
(Rom. 2:9-29) that the line which divides righteousness from wickedness does not coincide with national
differences between Jews and pagans. But paganism
as such, as an institution, with its religious errors
and moral depravities, is often still mentioned as a
special sphere of darkness and sin in opposition to
Christianity (Rom. 1:18-32; 1 Cor. 5:1; Eph. 4:17-19;
1 Thess. 4:5; cf. Gal. 2:15). This is quite understandable, because the first readers of the apostolic
writings had come mostly from paganism to Christianity, and this paganism was the type of life which
they had forsaken in order to convert themselves to
the light (2 Cor. 6:14-16; Eph. 5:8-14; Col. 1:12-13,
21; 1 Pet. 2:9-10).

According to these texts darkness may also be
found outside paganism, because they consider the
light to be the privilege of the one God of Israel.
Therefore Jews and pagans together find salvation
in Christ, which before had seemingly been reserved
for those who had received, with the Law, the
promises (Eph. 2:11-19). In contrast to this realm of
light the rest of the world is in darkness.

In other texts it is even more evident that, hearing
about spiritual darkness, we should not think ex-

clusively of paganism. In some texts there is not even an allusion to paganism (Mt. 5:14-16; Lk. 16:8; 1 Thess. 5:3-8). In others it is the Jews, or also the Jews, who are in darkness. Thus in Acts 26:17, 18 when Jesus says to Paul: "Having taken you from the people and from the Gentiles and sending you to them (or according to others: "Delivering you from the people and from the Gentiles to whom I send you") to open their eyes, that they may turn from darkness to light and from the power of satan to God." The words "to them etc." point also to "your people," the Jews. This is evident from Jesus' allusion in his explanation to the task of Jeremiah (Jer. 1:5-8) and especially to the task of the Servant of Yahweh (Is. 42:6-7). These prophetic missions concerned Jews as well as pagans. It is especially evident from the words which follow immediately, in which Paul relates to king Agrippa how faithfully he has carried out Jesus' order, and also from other reports about Paul's conversion and preaching (Acts 26:20; 9:15, 20-29; 13:5; 17:2). Saul therefore must be preacher and minister — also to the Jews — of that grace which he himself, a pharisee, received at the moment when, cured of his blindness, he converted himself to the light. Consequently these Jews are in darkness as long as they do not believe the gospel message of salvation.

We hear the same in some urgent exhortations of the Redeemer, which of course are true for everyone, but which were nevertheless directed to his Jewish hearers (Jn. 8:12; 12:35).

From all these texts it is evident that all people, Jews and pagans alike, come to the light only by becoming followers of Jesus. Only in the community of these followers, in the kingdom of God's beloved Son — in his Church — the light shines. Outside this community satan roams about with his angels, "the world rulers of this present darkness" (Eph. 6:12); this is the realm of darkness, continually waging war against the light. Those who respond to God's call, who accept the word of life, who by believing become Christ's disciples, who in baptism are incorporated into Christ and accepted into his Church, — they are the ones who receive forgiveness of sins and a heritage among the saints; they themselves can be called light and children of light (Mt. 5:1, 14; Jn. 12:35-36; Acts 26:18; Eph. 5:8; 1 Pet. 2:9).

They are children of light by virtue of a divine election and through the graces which have befallen them in Christ; but they are children also by virtue of a free choice, by which they accepted God's invitation, welcomed his grace, remained faithful to it.

2. Living as children of the light

The fact that the Christian freely responds to God's call explains why his light, in contrast to natural light, does not spread its splendor unconditionally. It is continually threatened by the darkness; it may allow itself to be assailed and overcome by this darkness. In other words, the Christian does not necessarily live as a Christian. From the moment that through faith and baptism he has adhered to

Christ there exists for him the possibility and the duty as a child of the light to let the splendor of his life spread its radiance.

The children of the light are insistently exhorted to let their light shine before men, in order that they could see their good works and glorify the Father who is in heaven (Mt. 5:14-16). They really must be children of the light and of the day, abandoning the works of darkness and putting on the armor of light, faith, hope and love (Rom. 13:12; 1 Thess. 5:5-8); they must walk as children of the light and take no part in the sterile works of darkness (Eph. 5:8-11). They must live blamelessly and innocently so that they will shine as the stars in the sky (Phil. 2:15). To incite their zeal they are told that the children of this world (in this case those who look after their worldly interests in a wrong way) act among themselves with more deliberation than do the children of light (Lk. 16:8).

Perhaps, too, the little parable of the eye being the lamp of the body (Mt. 6:22-23; Lk. 11:34-36) belongs to this series of exhortations. The meaning of this is not quite clear; but it could be as follows. We must take care that our eye, the lamp of our body, shines as a good lamp should; that it catches the light from outside and with it illuminates our body, ourselves, our conduct. There is also an inner lamp and we must take care that it catches the light of God's word and with it directs our person, our conduct in a Christian sense: that the flame in our heart is not extinguished by bad dispositions, willful blindness (Lk.), or covetousness of earthly goods (Mt.).

Finally, Paul points out how monstrous it is for a Christian not to live as a Christian: to form an unequal team with the unbelievers. "What fellowship has light with darkness?" (2 Cor. 6:14).

3. Believing in the light

Because a Christian way of life follows as a strict consequence from Christian existence, it is understandable that the fourth evangelist does not always mention it explicitly and that it sometimes looks as if it is sufficient to believe in the light which is Christ, or to follow that light (Jn. 8:12; 12:35-36). In fact this is not sufficient, if believing in the light or following the light is taken in the exclusive sense of accepting Christian doctrine. But it is sufficient in the sense in which the evangelist takes it, and in this sense the only important thing is man's attitude toward Christ. Believing in Christ and following Christ signify to John an unconditional surrender of one's whole personality to Christ. Faith in Christ can strike roots only in those who "do what is true" (Jn. 3:19-22), who practice the righteousness Christianity prescribes. For a Christian believing in the light and following it implicitly means to be a Christian and to live as a Christian.[23]

In fact no one has stressed more strongly than John

[23] According to Matthew 10:32-33 faith is sufficient; but, as Mt. 25:31-46 explains, it is a faith accompanied by practise of the virtues.

does that the light as a gift, like all graces of salvation, is at the same time an obligation. He knows that human weakness is bound to make itself felt in the life of a Christian (1 Jn. 2:1-2). Yet he writes: whoever walks in darkness, who does not try to avoid sin, nor to keep the new and the comprehensive command of the Lord, namely, the command of love, and who nevertheless pretends to be in communion with God, such a man is a liar, for "God is in the light" and even "God is light" (1 Jn. 1:5-8; 2:8-11). Such a man lacks exactly that which qualifies him to be a follower of Christ; like Judas he has torn himself loose from that community of life (Jn. 13:14-18, 30) which must radiate love, and in doing so must draw the rest of the world from darkness toward itself (Jn. 13:34-35; 15:10-17, 20-23).

12

LIGHT THROUGH

COMMUNION WITH THE LORD

There is therefore a strict commandment for the followers of Jesus to lead a pious life. But it is not true to say that Christianity is a light only because it demands a virtuous life from its followers. On the contrary, as is evident from the above texts, Christianity demands a virtuous life from its followers and requires them to walk as children of the light because Christianity itself is light. Christianity is light, and Christians become light in it, because of the special relationship which exists between them and Christ. The words of the apostle "Now you are light in the Lord" (Eph. 5:8) apply to the Church as a whole and to each of her children in particular.

1. The light of Christ

In the New Testament Christ is bearer of light, as he is bearer of glory. He is identified with light, which is not the case, at least not directly, with glory. In New Testament statements on this topic we usually find more or less clear references to texts of the Old Testament which indeed concern the mes-

sianic future, or texts — especially Prov. 8:22-31;
Wisd. 7:22; 8:1; Sir. 24:1-29 — in which the person
or the work of the Redeemer taught the disciples
to look for a deeper meaning.

The birth of Jesus is like the dawn of a bright
day, on which Yahweh appears in splendor to save
his people and to go before them in a luminous
cloud toward the promised land; and on it "his glory
fills the earth." Jesus (Yahweh saves) is his name,
"for he will save his people from their sins." A star
leads pagans, and the glory of the Lord which shone
about them leads the Jewish shepherds toward the
child which Mary[24] was allowed to give to the world
(Mt. 1:21; 2:2, 9-11; Lk. 2:9, 16-20).

As soon as Jesus begins his public life in Galilee
and announces the good news of the kingdom of
God, a prophecy is being fulfilled (Is. 8:23; 9:1
according to the Septuagint) about the saving day
of Yahweh, the day on which after the darkness of
calamity and exile the light of liberation and salvation dawns over God's people (Mt. 4:15-16). When
Zechariah, whose hymn of thanks is a composite of
biblical texts, describes the salvation of which his
son will be the forerunner (Lk. 1:76-79), he too is
thinking of this prophecy, but perhaps at the same
time of the prophecy of the Servant of Yahweh (Is.

---

[24] *Quae . . . virginitatis gloria permanente, lumen aeternum
mundo effudit, Jesus Christum Dominum nostrum* (Keeping
the splendor of her untouched virginity, she gave to the
world the eternal light, Jesus Christ our Lord) *Preface of
Our Lady.*

42:7) and of the messianic description of the future in Malachi (3:1, 20).

As the Son of Man is surrounded with glory when he appears on the clouds to pass divine judgment and to establish God's kingdom, so he is also enveloped in light (Acts 9:3; 22:6-11; 26:13); his victory on the day of judgment is accompanied by light (1 Cor. 4:5; 2 Pet. 1:19; cf. Rom. 13:11-13; 1 Thess. 5:4-8). In the transfiguration, which pre-reveals the glory of his resurrection and of his return, the light appears with the glory (Mt. 17:2, 5). That which radiates from the supreme judge on the last day will bring to light whatever was hidden in darkness, and make public whatever is in the hearts of men (1 Cor. 4:5). Although this is a terrifying prospect and although it exhorts everyone to serve God faithfully, yet the light of the triumphant Lord causes a splendor of happines and joy in his elect.

The revelation of splendor in the risen Redeemer is the crowning of his suffering; hence the disciples as a matter of course thought of the Servant of Yahweh. He was said to have been exalted so highly because of his laborious passion, he is "the covenant of the people and light unto the Gentiles" who radiates the salvation and the revelation of Yahweh to the ends of the earth. This is what Simeon said in his hymn (Lk. 2:30-32). This is what Paul said in his speech before Agrippa (Acts 26:23) and in his warning to the Jews in Antioch in Pisiadia, who refused to accept the word of God: "Behold, we turn to the Gentiles. For so the Lord has com-

manded us, saying: I have set you to be a light for
the Gentiles, that you may bring salvation to the
uttermost parts of the earth" (Acts 13:46-47). Even
though we might say that the apostle is applying
these words of Isaiah (49:6) to himself, which is
possible (cf. Acts 26:17-18), yet the light to the
Gentiles and the salvation of the whole world is
Christ, who speaks and acts in his apostle (cf. 2 Cor.
5:17-21; 13:3).

2. The inheritance of the saints in the light

At the end of the world the elect will appear as
participants of the Light of the Lord: "Then the
righteous will shine like the sun in the kingdom of
their Father" (Mt. 13:43). After life in this world, in
which the prophetic word, (Holy Scripture) is the
lamp which spreads light in a dark room (cf. Rom.
15:4) the new day dawns, and the morning star
(literally, the "bearer of the light," according to some
the morning star, according to others the sun) rises
in their hearts and expels all darkness (2 Pet. 1:19).

Paul possibly also speaks about the heavenly beati-
tude, in which he expects that the faithful will be
"with joy giving thanks to the Father, who has
qualified us to share in the inheritance of the saints
in the light" (Col. 1:12). But more probably he is
speaking about the grace of Christianity, because
he continues: "He has delivered us from the dominion
of darkness and transferred us to the kingdom of
his beloved Son, in whom we have redemption, the
forgiveness of sin" (Col. 1:13-14).

These two explanations do not differ very much. What is said about glory also holds true here. The New Testament knows of a participation in the light of the glorified Christ already during this earthly life. Indeed, if the prophecy about the Servant of Yahweh would be fulfilled — at least partly — and if the Lord be called light because of the light which radiates from him after his resurrection and which he will communicate to his followers on the day of judgment — these followers may, in this earthly life, be called "light and children of the light" because of that which will befall them only in the heavenly life. As is evident from what we have said before, the followers of Jesus do possess the gift of light in this life.

In fact, according to many texts of the New Testament, eschatological gifts or the blessedness of fulfillment came at Jesus resurrection. The faithful are already living in the first splendor of the day of Yahweh and of the final victory of the Lord (Rom. 13:11-12; 2 Cor. 4:6; Eph. 5:8; 1 Thess. 5:5). By baptism they have become participants of the light which radiates in the glorified Christ. Liberated from darkness and made citizens of the kingdom of heaven, they possess the inheritance of the saints in the light (Phil. 3:20; Col. 1:12-13). Having died with Christ and having risen to a new life, those who were darkness before are now light by their communion with the Lord, and children of the light. This is Paul's teaching. He finds a basis for it in a text which quite likely is part of an ancient baptismal

hymn and at the same time an allusion to Is. 9:1:
"Therefore it is said: Awake, O sleeper, and arise
from the dead, and Christ shall give you light"
(Eph. 5:8-14).

Baptism is an "enlightening" and a baptized man
is "enlightened" (Heb. 6:4; 10:32) because baptism
initiates one into the doctrine of Christ. Christ and
his doctrine can be called a light, as the forerunner
of the light is called a lamp (Jn. 5:35); or as a Jew,
according to Paul (Rom. 2:18), considers himself to
be "a guide to the blind, a light to those who are
in darkness," because he possesses the light of the
law. The Servant of Yahweh, whose mission it is to
teach law and morals to the people, is called "a light
to the nations" (Is. 42:1-6; 50:4-10). Jesus therefore,
continually appearing in the New Testament as
teacher, prophet, and herald of divine truth (Mt.
13:35; Lk. 4:17-24; Jn. 1:18; 3:11 etc.), realizes in his
person the prophecy of the Servant of Yahweh (Mt.
12:17-21); he is a light because of his preaching.

But the mission of the Servant of Yahweh is something more than preaching of truth. The doctrine
of Jesus is only part of the redemption he brings to
the world, or which he himself **is;** it is the complete
revelation of God's mercy, wisdom and love for
the world, expressed in the name light. If a baptized
man is said to be enlightened and if baptism is an
enlightening, these terms are used because he has
passed from the darkness of death into a new life,
because "he sees the light" and is assumed into the
light of the risen Lord.

In the second letter to Timothy the grace of
Christianity consists in sharing the light of the risen
Redeemer. The grace God communicated to us
from all eternity in Christ, has been made manifest
through the appearance — the incarnation (cf. Tit.
2:11; 3:4) — of the Redeemer; but only after his
victory over death does he make this imperishable
light dawn (2 Tim. 2:10). In the above quoted texts
of the apostle participation in the light of the risen
Redeemer constitutes the new light which is given
to man in baptism; the Lord gives him this life in and
through the Church. Jesus makes this imperishable
light dawn through the gospel of which the apostles
and those whom they appointed are the heralds (2
Tim. 1:8, 11; 2:1-3).

This light, which in heaven radiates in Christ and
on earth is in those who are baptized, is still hidden
from them. It is visible only to the eye of faith,
which sees even the invisible. But when in his second
coming the Lord descends from "the inaccessible light"
(1 Tim. 6:14-16) to refashion the body of our lowliness,
conforming it to the likeness of his own glorious
body, (Phil. 3:21), then we will see the light which
radiates in him and in ourselves.

13

JESUS THE LIGHT OF THE WORLD

The fourth gospel especially emphasizes the doctrine that Jesus brings light and is light himself. Only here is Jesus himself called the light. This evangelist repeatedly mentions or supposes the pre-existence of Christ; he also says that God is light. Hence we can ask ourselves if we must take this term in a theological sense as indicating the divine dignity and eternal pre-existence of the Word; or if we must take it in a soteriological meaning as indicating the incarnate Son in his redemptive mission and work.

1. Jesus called and calling himself the light

The prologue of the fourth gospel (Jn. 1:1-18) is a kind of Logos-hymn connected with the evangelical narrative proper by means of a few insertions about the mission of John the Baptist (Jn. 1:6-8, 15). In it the evangelist reveals the deep meaning of this narrative. The name light is very explicitly given to the Logos, the Word. We read: "All things were made through him (the Word), and without him was not anything made. That which has been made was

life in him (in the Word), and the life was the light
of men. The light shines in the darkness, and the
darkness has not overcome it" (Jn. 1:3-4). Scholars
do not agree about the punctuation and the translation of this text.[25] It is not possible to treat this exten-
sively here. Nearly all are of opinion that John
identifies the Word with life, and in turn, life with
light; for our purpose this is sufficient.

A little further, in contrast with John the Baptist,
who as forerunner and witness of the Lord, is called
"a burning and shining lamp" (Jn. 5:35), but not
"the light," it says: "The true light that enlightens
every man was coming into the world. He was in
the world, and the world was made through him,
yet the world knew him not" (Jn. 1:9-10).

In the evangelical narrative proper Jesus twice
calls himself "the light of the world" (Jn. 8:12; 9:5);
and it cannot be denied that in a few other state-

---

[25] "That which has been made was life in him." With the
variant reading "In what was made he (the Word) was the
life" "In what was made" means "in men." The rhythmic
flow of the prologue, in which the words of one part of the
sentence at the end form the beginning of the next part,
implies that the concept "men" is expressed in this way.
Moreover such indefinite expressions to indicate men are
not rare in John (Jn. 6: 6, 37-39; 10:29; 17:2). As to "be in"
with the meaning of "belong to," "be at the disposal of"
cf. Jn. 11:10; "the (sun) light is not in him"; 12:35; Mt. 6:23;
Lc. 11:35; cf. Jn. 14:30; the Lord of this world "has nothing
in me." However we admit that other explanations of
Jn. 1:3-4 are possible.

ments he makes about himself he applies light to himself (Jn. 3:19; 12:46).

Here we mention only that the word "world" in John has four or five different meanings, some of which are used in close proximity to one another, as in Jn. 1:9-10. The term may mean the universe, or the earth, or mankind, or more especially mankind as revelation shows it — mankind in as far as it is miserable and in need of God's mercy and Jesus' redemption (Jn. 1:29; 3:16) — or, finally, that part of mankind which persists in sin and refuses to be saved by Jesus (Jn. 15:18-19). In the texts in which Jesus is called the light of the world or in which it is said that the world did not acknowledge or accept the light, evidently it is not the cosmos which is meant, but, simply, mankind (cf. however Jn. 11:19 "the light of the world" i.e. the sun). This moreover is evident from the fact that John says as well: "the light of men" (Jn. 1:4) and "the true light that en- lightens every man" (Jn. 1:9).

2. The light which came into this world

It has at times been supposed that the name light in the gospel of John indicates the Word as a divine being or a divine person. The evangelist does say elsewhere: "God is light" (1 Jn. 1:5). In that case he would say exactly the same as the Nicene Creed (325) proclaims about Christ: "God from God, Light from Light, True God from True God." Possibly his intention might have been to place the Word as "the true light" in contrast to so called gods such as

Serapis, designated "a common light for all men," or
Isis, "a light for all mortals."[26]

Without a doubt the Nicene Creed is an exact
rendition of John's concept of Christ; the pagan gods
of light and sun would have been disgusting to him.
He had a firm faith in Christ's divinity, the foundation of all his statements about Jesus' person and
work. Yet those texts about the light are not a
testimony of this faith.

We have remarked that in the Old Testament light
never indicates the nature of a person. The same
is true in the New Testament. When John says that
"God is the light" (1 Jn. 1:7) and that "God is in the
light" (1 Jn. 1:7) it is clear from the context that he
wishes to impress upon his readers the absolute
holiness of God. In virtue of their Christian vocation they live in communion with Christ and through
him with God (1 Jn. 1:3), who lives in the light of
holiness and who is himself light of holiness without
any shadow of sin. How then would they walk in
darkness — lead a sinful life? Likewise, in another
text, John proceeds from an explanation (which also
is not a definition of God's being) that "God is love"
to an exhortation to practice sincere fraternal love
(1 Jn. 4:7-12, 16; cf. 1 Pet. 1:15, 22-23). Finally,

---

[26] Bauer, *Griechisches Worterbuch zu den Schriften des
Neuen Testaments 4*, Berlin 1952, s. v. — The formula
"Light of Light" to indicate that the Son proceeds in all
eternity from the Father, originated many years before the
council of Nicea (325). Cf. Rouet de Journel, *Enchiridion
Patristicum*, no. 609.

it is evident that God is in the light and that he himself is light because of the love which, in Christ, he radiates over the world: those who practice the great and all comprising command of Christian love share in the light and remain in the light (1 Jn. 2:3-11).

Wherever Christ is said to be light, it is evident from the context that it is not his divine nature which is meant; reference rather is made to his task or role with regard to mankind, in the world which he created and into which he came (Jn. 1:3, 10-11).

According to many scholars this is a task he fulfills before the incarnation and independent of it. As evidence of this they appeal to the first-mentioned gospel text (Jn. 1:4-5). The evangelist, they say, has just spoken about the share of the Word in the creation (verse 3); later (verse 6 ff.) he will speak about the mission of the forerunner and the appearance of God's Word in the flesh. Therefore his statement in verse 4 cannot possibly mean that the natural life of the world and the natural light of mankind (their intellectual understanding) hail from the Word. This would be a pale repetition of what he had already said so forcefully: "All things were made through him (the Word)." Thus far we can agree with their argument. But they go on: Neither can this statement refer to the role of the incarnate Word, which is only spoken of beginning with verse 6. Therefore it means that the Word, before the incarnation, was the source and origin of everything given to mankind by way of divine life and light. This however can be doubted.

It seems preferable to say that, here and every-
where in John, where Christ appears as light, the
incarnate Word is meant; so also is the salvation
which mankind obtains in him and through him.
The fact that the forerunner is mentioned in the
following verse does not prevent us from thinking
of the earthly mission of God's Son as already here.
John's thoughts usually do not develop themselves
in a straight line: they often present themselves as
a coherent and somewhat indefinite unit which shows
its different features in one or more slow revolutions,
and finally appears in a new formula in which,
clearly and in a single flash, all its lines are shown.
This is what happens here. The tremendous drama,
of which the whole fourth gospel is a description,
is first placed before us in general words (Jn. 1:4-5).
Afterward (Jn. 1:9-10) great stress is placed on its
significance and tremendous tragedy. Everything was
created by the Word. This Word became man:
Christ, "life and light" came from the Father in
order to bring salvation to sinful mankind. To this
sinful mankind, which is darkness, he continues
offering himself as the Redeemer: "The light shines
in the darkness." But "the darkness has not accepted
it" (according to a variant reading); he was rejected
by mankind created by him — rejected by "his own."

"The life which was the light of man" therefore
is Jesus Christ, the Incarnate Word. This he is, because he makes men share in the fullness which he,
the only begotten, receives from his Father; because
he brings them salvation. John the Baptist who as a
witness of the light may be called a lamp and who

gives light (Jn. 5:35), is not himself the light. No one except Christ is the true light (Jn. 1:9) because no one beside him is the salvation of the world.

Life and light in this context do not indicate two different entities but they mean salvation which appears in Christ, which he himself is; darkness and death, in contrast with this, indicate sin from which he saves mankind. Life is light as a joyful and bright reality. To readers familiar with the language of the Old Testament this way of speaking did not look strange at all.

3. The glorious light which dwells among men

The way in which the prologue speaks about Christ as light shows the influence of Wisdom literature, especially of the praises which are sung there to Wisdom personified or to the Word of God, which often show the same features. It is known that in the New Testament many pronouncements about Christ refer to them (1 Cor. 10:1-11; cf. Wisd. 10:17; 11:4; Col. 1:15-17; Heb. 1:3; cf. Prov. 8:22-23; Wisd. 2:25-26; Rev. 19:13-15; cf. Wisd. 18:14-18) especially in the fourth gospel (Jn. 4:14; 6:35; cf. Sir. 24:19-22 etc.). It is even probable that in these remarkable texts John found the model after which he fashions the stories of Jesus' words and works.[27] In any case, he

[27] One should remember that the fourth gospel develops itself as it were out of a few remarkable statements, in which the incarnate Word names himself, presents himself or testifies about himself: I am . . .; I have come . . . etc. The divine wisdom in many texts of the Wisdom books uses the same expressions.

had them in mind when he wrote his Logos-hymn.

The divine wisdom, operating in the creation of
the universe (Prov. 8:22-31; Wisd. 7:21; 8:1, 4-6;
Sir. 24:3; cf. Jn. 1:3), placed itself "in the book of the
covenant of the Most High" at the disposal of God's
people; she pitched her tent in the middle of God's
possession in order to dwell there as a source of
light and of life (Sir. 24:7-23, 32; Bar. 4:1). In a more
exalted way John sees all this realized in the incarnate Word (Jn. 1:14-18). Where in the former economy the law stood and the glory resided, here in the
new economy stands Jesus Christ in the glory which
he receives from the Father "full of grace and truth."[28]
Grace and truth: these are the gifts of redemption
for which we thank Christ. More especially, truth
means the entire divine revelation which appeared
to us in Christ: doctrine, duties and the cult which

---

[28] The words "grace and truth," literally "favor and fidelity" occur many times in the Hebrew Bible, indicating God's
faithfulness to his gracious covenant with Israel (Ex. 34:6;
Ps. 25:10; Os. 2:21) or God's constant benignity toward
his servants (Gn. 24:7; Ps. 40:11-12). In Ps. 43:3 as we saw
above (chapter V) the word favor is replaced by light
and in Ps. 57:4, 6, 11 and 12 steadfast love and faithfulness
are placed into close connection with God's glory as in
Exodus 33:18-23; 34:6 It is therefore probable that the
evangelist had this expression in mind when he wrote:
"grace (cnaris) and truth," though the Greek Bible in this
connection never translates the word favor by charis. But
evidently in that case John has given the words a new
meaning, as he did to light and glory, because he is
thinking here of Jesus and the redemption which appeared
in him and these he places far above, or even more or less
in contrast with, Moses and the law.

he established and which henceforth, in and through the Church, he renders to the Father (Jn. 4:23-26; 8:31-32; 17:3, 17-19; cf. Sir. 24:10-11).

Light here means the same as glory: an eschatological reality just like life or eternal life. What we have said about glory (chapter IX) is also true about light. It radiates in the risen Lord, but he already possessed it in an invisible manner from the moment of his incarnation. From him it flows into those who accept it, who believe in him. They already are, in a hidden manner, children of the light, children of God, risen from the dead, gifted with eternal life (Jn. 3:14-21; 5:24-27; 12:36). But one day the glorious resurrection will come: the radiant revelation of the light which on earth they possessed in the darkness of the faith, and eternal peace and joy with the Lord (Jn. 5:29; 6:39-40, 54; 11:24-26; 14:3; 1 Jn. 2:28; 3:2).

14

THE BLIND MAN WHO
MIRACULOUSLY SAW THE LIGHT

Besides the Wisdom books other biblical writings, in a lesser way, influenced the prologue, especially Is. 9:1 where mankind is described as seated in the darkness and the shadows of death. When Jesus in the gospel proper calls himself the light or reveals himself as such, this influence of Isaiah is even more pronounced.

1. The light which shines in the darkness

During his visit to Jerusalem on the occasion of the Feast of the Tabernacles, the divine Master declared: "I am the light of the world; he who follows me will not walk in darkness, but will have the light of life" (life as a radiating gift from God's goodness, Jn. 8:12). This may be an allusion to the luminous cloud (Ex. 13:21-22), by which the divine wisdom led the chosen people toward the promised land (Wisd. 10:17), as he too is a light that leads and is followed. But he certainly alludes to the text of Isaiah (Is. 9:1), just mentioned, which is also cited in the first gospel (Mt. 4:15-16); he refers to the light which the prophet saw rising over those who walk

in darkness and reside in the land and the shadows
of death.[29] The same is true of Jn. 3:19 and 12:46,
which show a remarkable similarity with what he
says in his prologue (Jn. 1:4-5, 9-11).

The light of life which those who follow the light
of the world will possess, is therefore, just as in
Matthew, the redemption which Isaiah announced for
the messianic times. As to the fact that Jesus calls
himself the light of the world, this reminds us of
the image of the Servant of Yahweh, which in a
pronounced way comes to the fore in the incomparable ninth chapter of John's gospel.

2. The light which makes the blind see

The entire ninth chapter of the gospel tells us
about the miraculous cure of the man born blind.
This moving story, in which we witness the light of
the world discharging its task, evokes very explicitly
the image of the Servant of Yahweh. About this
Servant was written (Is. 42:6; 49:6) that he was
appointed as a light to the gentiles, in order to open
the eyes of the blind and to release from their prison
those sitting in darkness.

[29] "Shadows of death" is the Septuagint translation of a
Hebrew word which really means profound darkness. Op-
posed to it is the light of life in Jn. 8:12. Our readers are
aware that the authors of the New Testament usually make
use of the Septuagint. But, as is evident from the vowel
signs of the Hebrew Bible, shadows of death is a case of
popular etymology of the Hebrew word current with the
Jews of Palestine, so that the allusion to Is. 9:1 in Jesus'
solemn statement was entirely intelligible to them. — This
short linguistic remark shows once more that for a Semite
darkness and death, light and life were cognate concepts.

Before curing the blind man, Jesus declares: "We must work the works of him who sent me, while it is day; night comes, when no one can work. As long as I am the world, I am the light of the world" (Jn. 9:4-5). He compares his life on earth to a day's work: "night, when no one can work" is for Jesus as well as for his hearers the hour of death. Of course he does not mean to say that he is the light of the world only as long as he remains in this world and that at his death and resurrection the world will be plunged into darkness again. What he means to say is that in fulfilling his task upon earth, he must reveal himself as the light of the world.

In order to do this he will work this miracle. The miracle therefore is a sign; not however an arbitrary sign, but a symbol: the outward action outlines in visible features what happens in the spiritual sphere and, as is often the case in biblical symbols, the outward action is a preparation for that spiritual event and makes it efficacious.[30] Jesus restores sight to the blind man, and in doing so he reveals that in him is realized what had been foretold about the

---

[30] A symbol in the Semitic world is "not a conventional or outward sign, but an objective reality. This real sign contains already effectively, and develops organically, a higher reality which at the same time is present in this sign and transcends it." C. Charlier, *Bijbellezen met de Kerk*, Roermond en Maaseik 1961, p. 302. On the biblical symbols confer also A. van den Born, *Profetie Metterdaad*, Roermond 1947. It goes without saying that the realism of the biblical symbol is an important item in the doctrine of the sacraments in Scripture. Compare with what we are to say about baptism in Jn. 9.

Servant of Yahweh: he is the light of the world, the
only one who cures the spiritual blindness of man
and liberates him from his spiritual darkness.

There is however one condition, expressed in the
circumstances of the miracle and also pointed out by
Jesus: the man who was cured bodily, was also
cured from his spiritual blindness because he fulfilled
this condition, while others — the pharisees in the
story, who were seeing — became blind. Only those
who realize the misery of their blindness, who are
really blind and in humble faith come to Jesus to
be cured, receive from him the gift of light. So it
happened to the cured beggar: he was blind, sought
to be cured and saw the light, the Son of Man (Jn.
9:35-38). Those however who refuse to acknowledge
their blindness, who see (claim to see) and who
therefore refuse to seek salvation with Jesus, remain
in the darkness of sin. So it happened to the
pharisees: they "saw," they made darkness "their
light" (Job 24:17; 38:15); therefore they "become
blind"; they fell into a blindness no longer open to
the light (Jn. 9:39-41; cf. 29).

The blind man who comes to the light and the
pharisees who refuse it show in advance what it is
that Jesus' work will bring about in the whole of
mankind. His appearance in this world as a light
constitutes a judgment; it splits mankind into two
parts: on one side are those who "did not see," but
become "seeing"; on the other side are those who
"saw" — thought themselves to see — and become
irretrievably "blind" (Jn. 9:39; cf. Jn. 1:9-13).

3. Meeting the light at the pool of Siloam

Some particulars of this story are intelligible only as an outline of a spiritual reality. Jesus, who is himself the light and wishes to reveal himself as the light which makes the blind see, cures the man born blind, not by means of a simple command or by an immediate touch. He puts the faith of the poor man to a severe test: "He spat on the ground and made clay of the spittle and anointed the man's eyes with the clay (which ordinarily would prevent a normal man from seeing), saying to him: Go, wash in the pool of Siloam (which means "Sent"). So he went and washed and came back seeing" (Jn. 9:6-7).

When the evangelist tells us that Siloam means "Sent" this evidently is not to display his knowledge of the language (for his etymology is not scientific[31]); he says it to teach us that the pool is a symbol of Jesus, eminently the "Sent One" (Jn. 3:17, 34; 5:36, 37, 38; 6:29 etc.). In this way the blind man finds Jesus again at the pool of Siloam where he had been sent and where he had gone in humble faith; and there in the water of the "Sent One" he receives the light of him who is the light of the world. Undoubtedly Augustine was right when he taught that this text teaches us the great mystery of holy baptism: when man is baptized in Christ, he receives the

[31] Probably the word originally means sender, discharger, waste pipe, drainage canal. The pool was situated at the end of a tunnel which carried the water from the Gichon-fountain. See B. Alfrink and J. Nelis, in *Bijbels Woordenboek 2*, c. 1578-1579.

light from the "light that enlightens every man."[32]
We have already seen (chapter XII) in what sense
baptism is an enlightening.

The cure of the blind man is a miracle and, as
miracles reveal the glory of Jesus (Jn. 2:11; 11:4, 40),
this revelation of the light teaches us again that the
light belongs to the glory of the Lord. That his
task as "resurrection and life" once more coincides
with both, is apparent also from the sign of the
raising of Lazarus (Jn. 11:1-44). Possibly the evangelist wished to point out this connection when on
the occasion of this miracle he mentions the remark
of some Jews: "Could not he who opened the eyes
of the blind man have kept this man from dying?"
(Jn. 11:37). Those who in the cure of the blind man
have not acknowledged Jesus as the light cannot,
for the same reason, understand that he is the
resurrection and the life. Because he is also the light
he vanquishes the greatest darkness, death, and
gives the light of life to those who believe in him
(Jn. 8:12; cf. 1:4).

[32] Augustine, *In Joannis Ev.*, tract. XLIV, 2.

CONCLUSION

All the goods and blessings of salvation which
God in the Old Testament promised for the messianic
time under the titles of glory and light — by which
he reveals the light of his infinite love and mercy —
were given to the world in Christ. He is the light
of the world, to be known in and through his Church.
How strikingly John described this tremendous
reality: the holy city Jerusalem, in which heaven and
earth meet, and which carries on its foundations the
twelve names of the twelve apostles of the Lamb.
"And the city has no need of sun and moon to shine
upon it, for the glory of God is its light, and its
lamp is the Lamb. By its light shall the nations
walk" (Rev. 21:14, 23-24).

"Let therefore everyone believe in the Church;
in her is the grace of the sevenfold Spirit. The
true high priest enlightens her with the splendor of
his sublime divinity, which the shadow of the law
may not darken . . . (The Church), the Jerusalem
which is in heaven . . . . has been placed upon the
highest of all mountains, on Christ. This Church cannot be buried beneath the darkness and the debris of
the world, but she radiates the splendor of the eternal
Son and enlightens us with the light of heavenly
grace."[33]

[33] Ambrose, *Expos. Ev. sec. Lucam*, VII, 98, 99.

The heavenly Jerusalem, the only Bride of the Lamb, is clothed and filled with God's glory. The Lord of glory, the light which enlightens every man, lives here. Those who through the word of his apostles believe in him, who remain in the community of love of which he is the bond — on them he radiates light of eternal light and makes them share in his glory so that they may be one and the world may know how much the Father loves them, in him.